George William Cox

Tales of the gods and heroes

George William Cox

Tales of the gods and heroes

ISBN/EAN: 9783742809933

Manufactured in Europe, USA, Canada, Australia, Japa

Cover: Foto ©Andreas Hilbeck / pixelio.de

Manufactured and distributed by brebook publishing software (www.brebook.com)

George William Cox

Tales of the gods and heroes

TALES

OF

THE GODS AND HEROES

BY THE

REV. GEORGE W. COX, M.A.

Late Scholar of Trinity College, Oxford

With 6 Illustrations on Wood from Designs by the Author

LONDON
LONGMAN, GREEN, LONGMAN, AND ROBERTS
1862

TO

HENRY REEVE, ESQ.

THIS VOLUME

IS

VERY GRATEFULLY INSCRIBED.

PREFACE.

THE progress of modern research has thrown a strange and unexpected light on the Mythology of the world. To the scholar or the philosopher, even of the last century, the fables of gods and deified heroes were things which deserved no thought at all; to less accurate thinkers they supplied the groundwork for a mass of crude and inconsistent speculation. To all their dreams, which saw, in the tales of Zeus or Poseidon or Athênê, either the medium for imparting a high esoteric morality or the expression of abstruse natural laws, the science of Comparative Mythology has, it would seem, dealt the death-blow. It has taught us that these old tales were no fancies devised by the restless Greek brain, and still less the result of a systematic attempt to build up a body of religious or moral belief. It has dispelled any idea that this collection of fables, to which the Hellenic mind imparted its own peculiar beauty, was by them handed on to the inhabitants of Italy, and presented to us under a harder and less genial form by the stern founders of the commonwealth of Rome.

This result it has achieved, not by argument and controversy, but by a simple exposition of facts. Those old tales whose beauty delights us in the poets of the Greek heroic ages, or which we find scattered through the dry pages of annalists and geographers, are proved to be the common inheritance of the whole Aryan race. Phœbus and Daphnê, Helios and Phaethon, are no longer the genuine growth of the Hellenic soil; Zeus and Heracles, Kephalos and Apollo, enter into the belief of the Magian and the Brahman not less than of the Roman and the Teuton. They may be traced further yet. The cannibal of Fiji places the abode of the dead in the land of the setting sun; and the legend of Pandora seems to be known to the wandering Indians of Labrador.

But on these common mythological stories each race or nation has impressed its own peculiar character. The legend of the Hindu breathes of the sleep-laden air of the tropics; the tales of the Norseman recount the giant conflicts of frost and fire. Yet if everywhere things shadowy or impersonal to us are in mythical speech invested with a real and even a personal life, the mythology of the Greeks has imparted to that personality a depth of human feeling which in its simplicity and truth appeals to the heart of man in every country and every age. So clear to us now is the origin and growth of many of these myths, that we are tempted to think that they also must have seen through the thin disguise which scarcely veils their real features. So readily do we see in the sorrows of Démétêr and the sleep of Endymion the interchange of day and night, of summer and winter, that we almost impute to them the same knowledge. Whatever may have been the conditions of an earlier age, it cannot have been thus in the days of Homer; yet even if it were, we should only have before us a stronger evidence of the strength of their human sympathy. We who have analysed the tales of Cadmus and Europa, of Orpheus and Eurydikê,—who have traced them from their first mythical stage to their complete personality,—yet feel that their joys and sorrows were such as are our own; and it is impossible that our feeling can be as keen and as intense as theirs. It is not only in their immortal epics that we find a human sentiment which exists as much now as it did then. It is seen in mere allusions or passing references to mythical beings, whose personality may be more than ordinarily thin and shadowy. The tragic poet who sympathised with the heavy toil and early death of that mighty being who filled so large a space of the mythical horizon, entered as deeply into the woes of the mother who wept for Itys, and the sorrow which turned Niobe to stone. Nay, he shared the grief or joy even where he had a half-consciousness that the beings of whom he sang were the sun above his head, and the earth on which he trod. And if we think that this imperfect consciousness ought to damp or repress the human feeling, we only show how utterly incapable we are of entering into a state of mind which once was that of the whole human race,— how little we are able to realise a fact which once was as really present as is our own age now. There was a time when, in place of the weakened consciousness of the later poets, men knew thoroughly that Dêmêtêr and Endymion were the Earth and the Sun; and the sympathy then felt for them, we might almost say shared with them, was even more intense and real.

Hence it is that their legends will delight the youngest child, as much as they still please those who have traced them back to their earliest form. In one sense, indeed, the child can appreciate them in a way which in later years he will never be able to recall, for his mind has not yet been awakened to an order of nature or to ideas of moral government; and the golden ram of Phrixus and the chariot of King Polydegmon are to him neither unnatural nor impossible. Any legend, therefore, in which the persons introduced may be spoken of simply as men and women, will be as readily understood by the youngest children as by those who are older. Some myths, which may throughout be treated thus, were collected in a volume entitled 'Tales from Greek Mythology.' But while the supernatural element, which is common to all, is no reason for withholding such tales even from children who can only hear them, it is obvious that the greater number of Greek myths involve ideas which either are very complicated, or else are distinctively heathen. Such ideas form no essential part of the stories of Niobe and Leto, of Selênê and Endymion; but the tales of Heracles, of Iô and Promêtheus, of Poseidon and Athênê, introduce us not merely to a world in which gods and men and deified heroes mingle together, but to wars and conflicts between gods and Titans, and to dynasties of gods fighting against and supplanting one another.

The Tales given in the present volume all involve more or less ideas of a kind which are likely to confuse and perplex a very young child. In some stories (as in those of Arethusa, Tyro, and Œnônê) it is impossible to keep out of sight the personality of rivers and mountains, in others (as Ariadne and Calypso) the union of undying gods with mortal men. But it is easy to lead the child who is acquainted with the simpler Tales to the knowledge that Dêmêtêr and Phœbus, Leto and Selênê, belong to the number of the deathless beings, and that Zeus had not always reigned on his Thessalian hill. With such a consciousness he may at once go on to these or other tales, which, if somewhat more complicated, yet appeal not less to feelings which the young and old alike may share, and with which none need ever be ashamed to sympathise.

In the following Tales but little has been introduced which may not be found in some one or other of the many versions of each legend. Those which belong to the Odyssey are faithfully given. The feeling of Homer needs no modification to adapt it to our own. With regard to the rest, a greater licence may perhaps be lawfully assumed. Some legends are not to be found anywhere as a whole; others, as they are given, are sometimes inconsistent; while many, even of the most beautiful, are not noticed in the great poems of the heroic ages. These, handed down in the common speech of the people, carry with them the surest evidence of their mythical origin, in the mere variety of forms into which they were thrown. But it is clear that of these versions some may depart more widely from the essential idea of the myth than others; and while amongst these we may fairly make our choice, others may be modified or altered, if only nothing is introduced which violates the one law of mythical credibility. That law is violated when Ovid makes Athênê appear unclad with Hêrê and Aphroditê, to receive the award of Paris.

From these old Hellenic legends the character of history has been torn away, if by history we mean the truthful record of things as they have been really done. The child will never again be taught that demigods and heroes were real men, over whose actions tradition has thrown a mist of poetry and romance. He will not be told that Erechtheus, and Minos, and Theseus were real kings, who reigned long ago in Athens or in Crete, —that the one put down piracy in the Ægæan Sea, while to the other is owing the settlement of Athenian society. He will no longer hear that Iphigeneia was the daughter of a chieftain who really led the hosts of Argos to do battle with the kinsfolk of Alexandros. But the very process which has stripped them of all value as a chronicle of actual events has invested them with a new and infinitely deeper interest. Less than ever are they mere idle tales to please the fancy or while away a weary hour; less than ever are they worthless fictions which the historian or philosopher may afford to despise. These legends, taken as a whole, present to us a form of society and a condition of thought through which all mankind had to pass long before the dawn of history. Yet that state of things was as real as the time in which we live. They who spoke the language of these early tales were men and women with joys and sorrows and interests here and hereafter not unlike our own. To turn aside from what they have to tell us is a cold and irrational selfishness; to examine their utterances carefully and patiently is nothing less than our bounden duty. Something they have to tell us of what men thought in times which could not be very far removed from the birth of the human race, of the aspects under which the outward world was presented to their eyes, of the relation which they felt to exist between themselves and the things or beings which they saw and felt on the earth and in the heavens. It is possible that such an examination may impart to us a knowledge which may bring with it both comfort and encouragement: it is idle to check it by uttering set phrases which may convey no meaning even to those who use them.

CONTENTS.

		PAGE
INTRODUCTION	. . . . .	1
I . . KEPHALOS AND PROCRIS	.	91
II . . DAPHNÊ	. . . .	105
III . . THE DELIAN APOLLO	.	108
IV . . THE PYTHIAN APOLLO	. .	110
V . . THE VENGEANCE OF APOLLO	. .	118
VI . . THE TOILS OF HERACLES	. . .	127
VII . . ALTHÆA AND THE BURNING BRAND	.	138
VIII . . PHAETHON	. . .	147
IX . . EPIMÊTHEUS AND PANDÔRA	.	150
X . . IÔ AND PROMETHEUS	. .	154
XI . . BRIAREÔS	. . .	162
XII . . SEMELÊ	. . . .	166
XIII . . PENTHEUS	. . .	169
XIV . . ARETHUSA	. . .	172
XV . . TYRO	. . .	175
XVI . . POSEIDON AND ATHENE	. .	178
XVII . . ARIADNÊ	. . .	183
XVIII . . NARCISSUS	. . .	190

		PAGE
XIX . . MEDEIA	. 192
XX . . ATHÊNÊ	. 198
XXI . . BELLEROPHON	. 201
XXII . . IPHIGENEIA	. 207
XXIII. . HECTOR AND ANDROMACHÊ	. 213
XXIV . . SARPÊDON	. 222
XXV . . MEMNON	. 228
XXVI . . ŒNÔNÊ	. 230
XXVII. . THE LOTOS-EATERS	. 245
XXVIII . THE CATTLE OF HELIOS	. 252
XXIX . . ODYSSEUS AND CALYPSO	. 263
XXX . . ATYS AND ADRASTOS	. 274

LIST OF ILLUSTRATIONS.

The Pillars of Heraclea. (Gibraltar from the Neutral Ground.) . *Frontispiece*

The Vale of the Peneios. Thessaly *To face page* 105

Marathon . 119

The Land of the Hesperides. (The African Coast from Gibraltar.) 133

The Land of Athênê. (The Hill of the Acropolis.) . 178

The Plains of Ilion . 230

TALES
OF
THE GODS AND HEROES.

INTRODUCTION.

Ὅσιον προτιμᾶν τὴν ἀλήθειαν.

THE Mythology of the Greeks presents, at first sight, as mysterious a problem as any that may perplex and bewilder even the soundest judgment. Their earliest extant literature exhibits a state of society which has long since emerged from mere brutishness and barbarism. It has its fixed order and its recognised gradations, a system of law with judges to administer it, and a public opinion which sets itself against some faults and vices not amenable to legal penalties. It brings before us men who, if they retain, in their occasional ferocity, treachery, and malice, characteristics which belong to the savage, yet recognise the majesty of law and submit themselves to its government,— who are obedient, yet not servile,— who care for other

[margin: Condition of society in the Greek heroic age.]

than mere brute forces, who recognise the value of wise words and prudent counsels, and in the right of uttering them give the earnest of a yet higher and more developed freedom.[1] It shows to us men who, if they regard all as enemies till by an outward covenant they have been made their friends, yet own the sanctity of an oath, and acknowledge the duty of executing true judgment between man and man,—who, if their life is passed in wars and battles, yet hold that the man who loves war deserves exclusion from law and hearth and clan[2],—who, if they are fierce in

---

[1] It cannot, of course, be maintained that this freedom was more than in its germ. The king has his Boulê or Council, where he listens to the chieftains whose judgment nevertheless he can override. There is also the Agora, where the people hear the determination at which their rulers have arrived, and in which justice is administered. The case of Thersites would imply a scanty right of opposition, while the complaints of Hesiod show that an unjust verdict could easily be obtained. But it was everything that a people should acknowledge Zeus to be the author of law,

δικασπόλοι . . . θέμιστας
πρὸς Διὸς εἰρύαται,   Il. i. 238.

and allow the force of mind over matter even in their chieftains. Mr. Grote has brought out the imperfections of the Homeric society both in discussion and administration of justice. (History of Greece, vol. ii. pp. 90—101.) Mr. Gladstone presents the picture in a more favourable light. (Homer and the Homeric Age, vol. ii. p. 122, &c.)

[2] ἀφρήτωρ, ἀθέμιστος, ἀνέστιός ἐστιν ἐκεῖνος
ὃς πολέμου ἔραται.   Il. ix. 63.

fight, yet abhor mutilation, torture, and unseemly insult, and are willing to recognise merit in an enemy not less readily than in a friend. Above all, it tells us of men who in their home life are honest and truthful, who make no profession of despising human sympathy and setting lightly by kindness, gentleness, and love. If here and there we get glimpses of a charity which seeks a wider range[1], yet the love of wife and children and brethren is the rule and not the exception; and everywhere, in striking contrast with Athenian society in the days of Pericles and Aspasia, we see men and women mingling together in equal and pure companionship, free alike from the arrogance and servility of Oriental empires, and from the horrible vices which, if even then in germ, were not matured till the heroic ages had long since passed away.[2]

But these epic poems tell us also of gods, some of whom at least had all the vices and few of the

---

[1] It is the praise of Axylos (who is slain by Diomedes) that
φίλος ἦν ἀνθρώποισιν·
πάντας γὰρ φιλέεσκεν ὁδῷ ἔπι οἰκία ναίων.
Il. vi. 14.

[2] To this more than to any other cause were owing even the political disasters of later Greek history. It may perhaps be said with truth that the evil did not exist in the Homeric age, but the canker had eaten very deeply into the heart of society before the days of Thucydides and Socrates. For its results see Dr. Thirlwall's History of Greece, vol. viii. ch. lxvi. p. 462, &c.

<small>Character of Homeric mythology.</small> virtues of their worshippers. They tell us of a supreme ruler and father of gods and men who had not always sat upon his throne, of other gods deposed and smitten down to dark and desolate regions, of feuds and factions, of lying and perjury, of ferocious cruelty and unmeasured revenge. They tell us of gods who delight in sensual enjoyments and care for little more than the fat of rams and goats, of gods who own no check to their passions and recognise no law against impurity and lust. And even those gods who rise to a far higher ideal, exhibit characters the most variable and actions the most inconsistent. The same being is at different times, nay almost at the same time, just and iniquitous, truthful and false, temperate and debauched. And over all, whether good or bad, hangs the doom which shall one day be accomplished; for the Olympian king, whose power had its beginning, is not to reign for ever.

The contrast is very marked between the character of the people and that of their theology, <small>Contrast between mythological and religious belief.</small> if in any sense the latter deserves the name; nor can it be said that they were unconscious of the contrast. It is impossible for us to determine the extent to which that theology was believed, because it is not in our power to throw ourselves back wholly into their condition of thought; but if the absence of all doubt or reflection constitute faith, then their faith was given to the whole cycle of fables which made up the chronicles of their gods. But if we look to its influence on their practice, we can scarcely say that this huge fabric of mythology challenged any belief at all. If the poet recounts the loves of Zeus, the jealousies of Hêrê, the feuds and the factions in Olympus, it is equally certain that Achilles does not pray to a sensual and lying god who owns no law for himself and cannot be a law for man.[1] The contrast is heightened as we come down to a later age. If the poet narrates a theogony which drew on itself the detestation or disgust of Pindar and of Plato, he tells us also of a Divine King who is a perfectly upright judge and loves those who are clean of hand and pure of heart.[2] If he tells of horrible banquets to which the more fastidious

---

[1] See more particularly Max Müller's Comparative Mythology, in Oxford Essays for 1856, pp. 7—10. I would here acknowledge my deep obligation to Professor Müller, for instruction gained from his most valuable works on the subjects of Mythology and the Science of Language.

[2] The identity of authorship for the Theogony and the Works and Days of Hesiod is very doubtful; but the question is immaterial. Both poems exhibit the sentiment of the same age, or of times separated by no great interval. And in the latter poem the action of Zeus in the legend of Pandora (which is also related in the Theogony) is utterly unlike the Zeus who figures in all the didactic portions of the work.

faith of a later poet refuses to give credence[1], he bids all to follow after justice because the gods spend their time not in feasting, but in watching the ways and works of men.[2] If Æschylus in one drama depicts the arrogant tyranny of Zeus as a usurper and an upstart, if the reiterated conviction of the prophetic Titan is that the new god shall fall, yet in others he looks up to the same Zeus (if indeed it be the same [3]) as the avenger of successful wrong, the vindicator of a righteous law, whose power and goodness are alike eternal. If for Sophocles the old epic mythology had not lost its truthfulness and its charm, if he too might have told of the lawless loves and wild licence of Zeus and other gods, yet his heart is fixed on higher realities, on that purity in word and deed which has its birth not on earth but in heaven, and of which the imperishable law is realised

[1] ἐμοὶ δ᾽ ἄπορα γαστρίμαρ-
γον μακάρων τιν᾽ εἰπεῖν· ἀφίσταμαι.
Pindar, Olymp. i. 82.

Pindar's objection is a moral one; but Herodotus proceeded to reject on physical grounds the legend which told of the founding of the Dodonæan oracle (ii. 57), as well as some of the exploits of Heracles (ii. 45). It was, however, a moral reason which led him practically to disbelieve the whole story of Helen's sojourn at Troy (ii. 120). See also Grote, History of Greece, vol. i. p. 416, &c.

[2] Works and Days, 247—253.

[3] Ζεὺς ὅστις ποτ᾽ ἐστίν.
Agamemnon, 160.

and consummated in a God as holy and everlasting.¹

It would be difficult to discover a more marvellous combination of seemingly inexplicable contradictions, of belief in the history of gods utterly distinct from the faith which guided the practice of men, of an immoral and impure theology with a condition of society which it would be monstrous to regard as utterly and brutally depraved. Yet, in some way or other, this repulsive system, from which heathen poets and philosophers learnt gradually to shrink scarcely less than ourselves, had come into being, had been systematised into a scheme more or less coherent, and imposed upon the people as so much genuine history. What this origin and growth was, is (strange as it may appear) one of the most momentous questions which we may put to ourselves, for on its answer must depend our conclusions on the condition of human life during the infancy of mankind. If the fragmentary narratives which were gradually arranged into one gigantic system, were the work of a single age or of several generations who devoted themselves to their fabrication, then never has there been seen in the annals of mankind an impurity more loathsome, an appetite more thoroughly depraved,

¹ Œd. Tyr. 863—871.

a moral sense more hopelessly blunted, than in those who framed the mythology of the Greeks. Of the answers which have been given to this question, it can be no light matter to determine which furnishes the most adequate solution.

The method which Mr. Grote, in his History of Greece [1], has adopted for the examination of Greek legend, appears rather to avoid the difficulty than to grapple with it. There is unquestionably much personification in their mythology; there is also undoubtedly a good deal of allegory; but neither allegory nor personification will furnish a real explanation of the whole. It may be true to say that Ouranos, Nux, Hupnos, and Oneiros are persons in the Theogony of Hesiod, although it is probably erroneous to say that they are just as much persons as Zeus or Apollo; and the supposition is certainly inadmissible 'that these legends could all be traced by means of allegory into a coherent body of physical doctrine.' [2] But there are beyond doubt many things even in the Theogony of Hesiod which have at least no human personality [3]; nor does

[marginal note: Historical significance of Greek mythology]

---

[1] Vol. i. chaps i. xvi.

[2] Grote, History of Greece, vol. i. pp. 2, 3. See also Mure, Critical History of Greek Literature, vol. i. p. 104, &c. Milman, History of Christianity, vol. i. p. 13, &c.

[3] For instance, οὐρία μακρά. Theog. 129. See Professor Max Müller, Comparative Mythology, p. 41.

the assertion of personality, whether of Zeus or Heracles or Apollo, in the least degree account for the shape which the narrative of their deeds assumes, or for the contradictory aspects in which they are brought before us. It does not in any way explain why Zeus and Heracles should have so many earthly loves, and why in every land there should be those who claim descent from them, or why there should be so much of resemblance and of difference between Phœbus and Helios, Gaia and Demeter, Nereus and Poseidon. But Mr. Grote was examining the mythology of Greece as an historian of outward facts, not as one who is tracing out the history of the human mind; and from this point of view he is justified in simply examining the legends, and then dismissing them as the picture 'of a past which never was present.' To this expression Professor Max Müller takes great exception, and especially protests against Mr. Grote's assertion of 'the uselessness of digging for a supposed basis of truth' in the myths of the Greek world.[1] But although it appears certain that the Greek mythology points to an actual and not an imaginary past, a past which must have for us a deep and an abiding interest, it would yet seem that Professor Müller has misinterpreted the words of Mr. Grote,

---

[1] Comparative Mythology, pp. 1, 41, 52.

who by 'truth' means the verification of actual occurrences, and by a real past means one of whose events we can give an authentic narrative.[1] In this sense to assert the truth of the lives and adventures of Zeus and Heracles is to fall back on the system of Euêmerus, and to raise a building without foundation. But it is obvious that this method leaves the origin of this theology and the question of its contradictions, and still more of its impurity and grossness, just where it found them. It carries us no further back than the legends themselves, while it fails to remove the reproach which heathen apologists and Christian controversialists alike assumed or admitted to be true.[2]

Two theories only appear to attempt a philosophical analysis of this vast system. While one repudiates the imputation of a deliberate fabrication of impurities, the other asserts

<small>Conflicting views as to its origin.</small>

[1] From this point of view it is impossible to deny the truth of Mr. Grote's statement, when, speaking of the Northern Eddas, he says that, 'the more thoroughly this old Teutonic story has been traced and compared in its various transformations and accompaniments, the less can any well-established connection be made out for it, with authentic historical names or events.'—*History of Greece*, vol. i. p. 642. It is strange that, having thus swept away its historical character, he should not have seen that there *must* be some reason for the singular agreement between Teutonic and Greek mythology, which at the least he partially discerns, p. 640, &c.

[2] Grote, History of Greece, vol. i. p. 565, &c.

as strongly the wilful moral corruption exhibited in the theogonic narratives of the Greeks. In the inconsistent and repulsive adventures of Zeus or Heracles, it sees the perversion of high and mysterious doctrines originally imparted to man, and discerns in the gradations of the Olympian hierarchy vestiges of the most mysterious truths which form the subject of Christian belief. By this theory all that is contradictory, immoral, or disgusting in Greek mythology is the direct result of human sinfulness and rebellion, and resolves itself into the distortion of a divine revelation imparted to mankind in the patriarchal age.

There are few subjects in which it would be more rash to give or withhold assent to any statement without the clearest definition of terms. We may admit the truth of Bishop Butler's assertion that the analogy of nature furnishes no presumption against a revelation when man was first placed upon the earth [1]; but it is obvious that those who agree in asserting the fact of such a revelation may yet have widely different conceptions of its nature and extent. And although it is easy to see the place which Bishop Butler's statement holds in the general connection of his argument, it is not so easy to ascertain what on this point his own judgment

Hypothesis of an original revelation.

[1] Analogy, Part II. ch. ii. § 2.

may have been. Human feeling recoils instinctively from any notion that the Being who placed man in the world ever left him wholly to himself; but the repudiation of such an idea in no way determines the amount of knowledge imparted to him at the first. Nations have been found, and still exist, whose languages contain not a single word expressive of divinity, and into whose mind the idea of God or of any religion appears never to enter.[1] Yet if we accept as a fact that original unity of the human race and species, to which the analysis of language [2], the stores of a common mythology [3], and the progress of physical science [4] seem alike to point, we can scarcely suppose that from the first the condition of such nations has undergone no change whatever. It is hard to measure

---

[1] 'Penafiel, a Jesuit theologian, declared that there were many Indians who, on being asked whether during the whole course of their lives they ever thought of God, replied, *no, never.*'—*Max Müller, History of Sanskrit Literature*, p. 538.

[2] Professor Max Müller, in his Lectures on the Science of Language (p. 316, &c.), has shown that the analysis of language furnishes no presumption against an original unity of all languages. But although he denies any necessary connection of the subject with that of unity of race, his own answer appears to be in the affirmative to both.

[3] For a summary of the arguments on the diffusion of the Aryan mythology, see Dasent, Popular Tales from the Norse, Introduction, pp. xxxi.—lv.

[4] See the conclusions of M. Quatrefages, Unité de l'Espèce Humaine.

the depth of degradation to which the Abipones, the Bushman, and the Australian may have fallen; it is impossible to believe that the struggles of men like Socrates and Plato after truth had no connection with a guiding and controlling power. If in the former we cannot refuse to see the evidence of a wilful corruption, we must recognise in the latter the vigorous growth of a mind and spirit which seeks to obey the law of its constitution.[1] In Bishop' Butler's philosophy, the reason of man is the Divine Reason dwelling in him; the voice of his conscience is the word of God. That these gifts conveyed with them a revelation of divine truth, it is impossible to deny; but it is unlikely that by the assertion of an original revelation Bishop Butler meant no more than this. The Analogy affords no further answer to the question; but if we are still left to determine the extent of that revelation, we cannot lay too much stress on his assertion that the question is to be considered 'as a common question of fact.'[2]

No such charge of ambiguity can be brought against the view which Mr. Gladstone has maintained in his elaborate work on Homer and the Homeric Age. In his judgment all that is evil in Greek mythology is the result

Extent of original revelation.

---

[1] Butler, Sermons:—II. On Human Nature.
[2] Analogy, Part II. ch. ii. § 2.

not of a natural and inevitable process, when words used originally in one sense came unconsciously to be employed in another, but of a systematic corruption of very sacred and very mysterious doctrines. These corruptions have, in his opinion, grown up not around what are generally called the first principles of natural religion, but around dogmas of which the images, so vouchsafed, were realised in a long subsequent dispensation. In the mythology of the Hellenic race he sees a vast fabric, wonderfully systematised, yet in some parts ill cemented and incongruous, on the composition of which his theory seems to throw a full and unexpected light. In it he hears the key-note of a strain whose music had been long forgotten and misunderstood, but whose harmony could never of itself have entered into mortal mind. It could not be supplied by invention, for 'invention cannot absolutely create; it can only work on what it finds already provided to hand.'[1] Rejecting altogether the position that 'the basis of the Greek mythology is laid in the deification of the powers of nature,'[2] he holds that under corrupted forms it involves the old Theistic and Messianic traditions[3], that by a primitive tradition, if not by a direct com-

[1] Homer and the Homeric Age, vol. ii. p. 9.
[2] Ibid. p. 10.
[3] Ibid. p. 12.

THEORY OF CORRUPT DEVELOPMENT

mand, it upheld the ordinance of sacrifice [1], that its course was from light to darkness, from purity to uncleanness.[2] Its starting point was 'the idea of a Being infinite in power and intelligence, and though perfectly good, yet good by an unchangeable internal determination of character, and not by the constraint of an external law.'[3] But the idea of goodness can only be retained by a sound moral sense; the notion of power is substituted when that sense is corrupted by sin.[4] But sin has no such immediate action on the intellect. Hence the power and wisdom of the Homeric gods is great and lofty while their moral standard is indefinitely low.[5] But the knowledge of the Divine Existence roused the desire to know also where He dwelt; and in the mighty agencies and sublime objects of creation, in which they fancied that they saw Him, Mr. Gladstone sees the germs of that nature-worship which was ingrafted on the true religion originally imparted to mankind.[6] This religion involved [7] (1.) the Unity and supremacy of the Godhead; (2.) a combination, with this Unity, of a Trinity in which the

---

[1] Homer and the Homeric Age, vol. ii. p. 15.
[2] Ibid. p. 17. 'The stream darkened more and more as it got further from the source.'
[3] Ibid. p. 18.
[4] Ibid. p. 19.   [5] Ibid. p. 20.
[6] Ibid. p. 31. [7] Ibid. p. 42.

several Persons are in some way of coequal honour; (3.) a Redeemer from the curse of death, invested with full humanity, who should finally establish the divine kingdom; (4.) a Wisdom, personal and divine, which founded and sustains the world; (5.) the connection of the Redeemer with man by descent from the woman. With this was joined the revelation of the Evil One, as a tempting power among men, and the leader of rebellious angels who had for disobedience been hurled from their thrones in heaven.

Putting aside the question how far these ideas may not reflect the thought of later ages, we must admit with Mr. Gladstone that from this shadowing forth of the great dogmas of the Trinity and the Incarnation, the next step might be into polytheism, and from that of the Incarnation into anthropomorphism, or the reflection of humanity upon the supernatural world.[1] This true theology, in the hands of the Greeks, was perverted into a trinity of the three sons of Kronos,— Zeus, Hades, and Poseidon. The tradition of the Redeemer is represented by Apollo, the Divine Wisdom is embodied in Athênê[2]; and Lêtô, their mother, stands in the place of the woman from whom the Deliverer was to descend. The traditions of the Evil One were

Its alleged perversion by the Greeks.

---

[1] Homer and the Homeric Age, vol. ii. p. 43. [2] Ibid. p. 44.

still further obscured. Evil, as acting by violence, was represented most conspicuously in the Titans and giants — as tempting by deceit, in the Atê of Homer; while, lastly, the covenant of the rainbow reappears in Iris.[1]

For these primitive traditions which are delivered to us 'either in the ancient or the more recent books of the Bible,'[2] Mr. Gladstone alleges the corroborative evidence furnished by the Jewish illustrative writings during or after the captivity in Babylon.[3] These writings bear witness to the extraordinary elevation of the Messiah, and to the introduction of the female principle into Deity, which the Greeks adopted not as a metaphysical conception, but with a view to the family order among the immortals.[4] Thus in the Greek Athênê and Apollo respectively he distinguishes the attributes assigned by the Jews to the Messiah and to Wisdom, the attributes of sonship and primogeniture, of light, of mediation, of miraculous operation, of conquest over the Evil One, and of the liberation of the dead from the power of hell, together with 'an assemblage of the most winning and endearing moral qualities.'[5]

as shown in the attributes of their gods.

This theory Mr. Gladstone has traced with great

---

[1] Homer and the Homeric Age, vol. ii. p. 45.   [2] Ibid. p. 48.
[3] Ibid. p. 50.   [4] Ibid. p. 51.   [5] Ibid. p. 53.

minuteness and ingenuity through the tangled skein of Greek mythology. The original idea he finds frequently disintegrated, and a system of secondaries is the necessary consequence. Far above all are exalted Apollo and Athênê, in their personal purity[1] yet more than in their power, in their immediate action[2], in their harmony to the will of the supreme king, and in the fact that they alone among the deities of a second generation are admitted to equal honour with the Kronid brothers, if not even to higher.[3] But some of their attributes are transferred to other beings, who are simply embodiments of the attribute so transferred and of no other. Thus Athênê is attended by Hermes, Ares, Themis, and Hephæstos, Apollo by Paieon and the Muses[4]; as, similarly, we have in Gaia a weaker impersonation of Dêmêtêr, and Nereus as representing simply the watery realm of Poseidôn. In Lêtô, their mother, is shadowed forth the woman whose seed was to bruise the head of the serpent; for Lêtô herself has scarcely any definite office in the Homeric theology, and she remains, from any view except this one, an anomaly in mythological belief.[5] But the traditions which relate to the under world, which is the realm of Hades, are not less full than those

Marginal note: System of secondaries.

[1] Homer and the Homeric Age, vol. ii. pp. 87, 107.
[2] Ibid. pp. 89—93.   [3] Ibid. p. 57.
[4] Ibid. p. 61.   [5] Ibid. p. 152.

which tell us of the heavenly order of Olympus. Amidst some little confusion Mr. Gladstone discerns a substantial correspondence with divine revelation, and finds in the Homeric poems the place of bliss destined finally for the good, the place of torment inhabited by the Evil One and his comrades, and the intermediate abode for departed spirits, whether of the good or the evil.[1] But while the prevalence of sacrifice attests the strength of primitive tradition, of the Sabbatical institution there is no trace.[2] It was an ordinance 'too highly spiritual to survive the rude shocks and necessities of earthly life.'

Of the other deities some owe their existence to invention, which has been busy in depraving and debasing the idea even of those which are traditive.[3] Thus Hêrê was invented because Zeus must not live alone, and Rhea because he must have a mother; and a whole mass of human adventure and of human passion, without human recognition of law, is heaped up round almost every deity (except the two who stand out unsullied in their purity and goodness), not however without occasional protests from the poet who had not yet become familiar with the deification of vicious passion.[4]

Inventive as distinguished from traditive deities.

[1] Homer and the Homeric Age, vol. ii. p. 170.
[2] Ibid. pp. 171, 172.   [3] Ibid. p. 173.   [4] Ibid. p. 270.

Thus, on the hypothesis of Mr. Gladstone, Greek mythology is no distortion of primary truths which first dawn on the mind of a child or are imparted to it, and which, it might have been supposed, would form the substance of divine truth granted to man during the infancy of his race. It is the corruption of recondite and mysterious dogmas, which were not to become facts for hundreds or thousands of years, of doctrines which the speculations of Jewish rabbis may have drawn into greater prominence, but which form the groundwork of Christian theology. Zeus, the licentious tyrant, the perjured deceiver, the fierce hater, the lover of revelry and banqueting, who boasts of his immunity from all restraint and law, is the representative of the Infinite and Eternal God. He, with Hades and Poseidon, represents the Christian Trinity; but Hades represents also the power of darkness, and Poseidon shares the attributes of God with those of the devil [1], while all are born of the dethroned Kronos, in whom again the evil power finds an impersonation.[2] When we survey the whole mass of mythological legend, when we spread out before us the lives of Zeus and his attendant gods (scarcely excepting even Athênê and Apollo), we stand aghast at the

---

[1] Homer and the Homeric Age, vol. ii. p. 164.   [2] Ibid. p. 207.

boldness of an impiety which has perhaps never had its parallel. The antediluvian records of the Old Testament bring before us a horrible picture of brute violence, resulting possibly from a deification of human will which, it would seem, left no room for any theology whatever; but this is a very rioting in profanity, a monstrous parody which would seem to be founded not on dim foreshadowings of a future revelation, but on the dogmatic statements of the Athanasian creed. That a theology thus wilfully falsified should be found with a people not utterly demoralised, but exhibiting on the whole a social condition of great promise and a moral standard rising constantly higher, is a phenomenon, if possible, still more astonishing. On the supposition that Greek mythology was a corrupted religious system, it must, to whatever extent, have supplied a rule of faith and practice, and the actions and character of the gods must have furnished a justification for the excesses of human passion. That no such justification is alleged, and that the whole system seems to exercise no influence either on their standard of morality or their common practice, are signs which might appear to warrant the presumption that this mythology was not the object of a moral belief. The whole question as viewed in this light is so utterly perplexing, and, apparently, so much at variance with the conditions of Homeric society, that we are driven to examine more strictly the evidence on which the hypothesis rests. We remember that we are dealing not with a theme for philosophical speculation, but with a common question of fact.[1]

If once the hypothesis be admitted, then it must be granted that the attributes and functions of the Hellenic gods have seldom been analysed with greater force, clearness, and skill; nor is it possible to deny that that hypothesis, as in the case of Lêtô, explains much which would otherwise appear anomalous. At the least it furnishes a plausible interpretation of many points which may yet be susceptible of another treatment.[2] But it introduces the necessity of interpreting mythology so as to square with a preconceived system, and involves a temptation to lessen or to pass over difficulties which appear to militate against it. The Homeric legends are not so consistent as for such a purpose would seem desirable; and there are the gravest reasons for

Attributes of Athênê and Apollo.

---

[1] See page 13.
[2] Mr. Gladstone (Homer, &c. vol. ii. p. 155) dwells much on the indistinct colouring which is thrown over Leto, and which leaves her 'wholly functionless, wholly inactive,' and 'without a purpose,' except in so far as she is the mother of Phœbus. But this is precisely the relation in which the mythical Night stood to the Day which was to be born of her. It was impossible that the original idea could be developed into a much more definite personality. See page 49, and note 1, p. 69.

not inferring from the silence of the poet that he was ignorant of other versions than those which he has chosen to adopt.[1] On the supposition that Athênê and Apollo represent severally the Divine Redeemer and the Divine Wisdom, their relation of will to the Supreme Father becomes a point of cardinal interest and importance. But when Mr. Gladstone asserts that, although Athênê 'goes all lengths in thwarting Jupiter' in the Iliad[2], 'yet her aim is to give effect to a design so unequivocally approved in Olympus, that Jupiter himself has been constrained to give way to it,' he places too far in the background certain other Homeric incidents which imply a direct contrariety of will. No weaker term can rightly characterise the abortive conspiracy to bind Zeus, in which she is the accomplice of Hêrê and Poseidon. In this plot, the deliverance comes not from Apollo, whose office it is to be 'the defender and deliverer of heaven and the other immortals,' but from Thetis, the silver-footed nymph of the sea[3]; and

[1] See page 66.
[2] Gladstone's Homer, &c. vol. ii. p. 70.
[3] Ibid. p. 72. The conspiracy so crushed is mentioned more than once by Mr. Gladstone (pp. 75, 182); but he mentions it, not as a drawback on the traditive character of Athênê, but as showing first that Zeus himself might be assailed, and secondly that his majesty remained nevertheless substantially unimpaired. Yet a reference to it, as bearing on the moral conception of Athênê, would seem to be indispensable.

by her wise counsels Zeus wins the victory over one who is with himself a member of the traditive Trinity. This same legend qualifies another statement, that Athênê and Apollo are never foiled, defeated, or outwitted by any other of the gods[1]; for Athênê here is foiled by Thetis. Elsewhere we have Apollo[2], like Poseidon, cheated by Laomedôn, whom he had served, and finding a more congenial master, but yet a master, in Admetos[3], while the parentage of the three Kronid brothers[4] and the double character of Poseidon[5] stand forth as the most astounding contradictions of all.

[1] Gladstone's Homer, &c. vol. ii. p. 74.
[2] Ibid. p. 75.
[3] Ibid. p. 81. If these legends are regarded strictly as corruptions of old mythical phrases, there is no difficulty whatever in such statements. In them there is reflected upon Apollo an idea, derived from the toiling sun, which is brought out in its fulness in the adventures of Heracles and Bellerophon. Mr. Gladstone lays much stress on the relation of Apollo and Artemis to Death (p. 103), and holds that here we are on very sacred ground (p. 104), the traces, namely, 'of One who, as an all-conquering King, was to be terrible and destructive to his enemies, but who was also, on behalf of mankind, to take away the sting from death, and to change its iron band for a thread of silken slumber.' The question is further examined (p. 23, &c.); but the myths developed from phrases which spoke originally of the beneficent and destructive power of the sun's rays and heat, perfectly explain every such attribute whether in Apollo or Artemis.
[4] Gladstone, Homer, &c. vol. ii. p. 162.
[5] Ibid. p. 206.

There are other legends which represent Athênê in a light inconsistent with the personification of the Divine Wisdom. In the tale of Pandora, at the instigation of Zeus she takes part in the plot which results in the increased wickedness and misery of man[1]; in that of Prometheus, she aids in the theft of fire from heaven against the will of Zeus, while one version represents her as acting thus not from feelings of friendship, but from the passion of love. These legends are not found in Homer, but it is impossible to prove that he was unacquainted with them. He makes no reference to some myths which are at once among the oldest and the most beautiful; and he certainly knew of the dethronement of Kronos, as well as of factions in the new dynasty of the gods.[2]

Relations of will between Athênê and Zeus.

But if the theory of religious perversion, apart from its moral difficulties, involves some serious contradictions, it altogether fails to explain why the mythology of the Greeks assumed many of its peculiar and perhaps most striking features. It does not show us why some of the gods should be represented as pure, others

Peculiar forms of Greek mythology.

---

[1] Hesiod. Theogon. 573. Works and Days, 63.

[2] Similarly, he is silent as to the death of Achilles, yet he is aware that his life is to be prematurely closed.

μῆτερ, ἐπεί μ' ἔτεκές γε μινυνθάδιόν περ ἐόντα,

is the reproach of Achilles to his mother Thetis.

as in part or altogether immoral; it does not tell us why Zeus and Heracles should be coarse and sensual, rather than Athênê and Apollo; it does not explain why Apollo is made to serve Admetos, why Heracles bears the yoke of Eurystheus, and Bellerophon that of the Kilikian king. It fails to show why Heracles should appear as the type of self-restraint and sensuality, of labour and sluggishness, why names so similar in meaning as Phœbus, Helios, and Phaethon, should be attached to beings whose mythical history is so different. If for these and other anomalies there is a method of interpretation which gives a clear and simple explanation of them, which shows how such anomalies crept into being, and how their growth was inevitable,—if this method serves also as a key not merely to the mythology of Greece, but to that of the whole Aryan race, nay, even to a wider system still,—a presumption at least is furnished that the simpler method may after all be the truest.

Yet more, the hypothesis of a corrupted revelation involves some further consequences which have a material bearing on the question. That which is so perverted cannot become clearer and more definite in the very process of corrupt development. Not only must the positive truths, imparted at the first, undergo distortion, but the ideas involved

Consequences involved in the perversion of an original revelation.

in them must become weaker and weaker. If
the Unity of God formed one of those primitive
truths, then the personality and the power of
Zeus would be more distinct and real in the
earliest times than in the later. The ideas of the
Trinity, of the Redeemer, and of the Divine Wisdom, would be more prominent in those first stages
of belief in the case of a people who confessedly
were not sustained by new or continued revela-
tions. The personality of a Divine Wisdom is
not a dogma which men could reason out for
themselves; and if it formed part of an original
revelation, the lapse of time would tend to weaken,
not to strengthen it. And if again this corrupt-
ing process had for its cause a moral corruption
going on in the hearts and lives of men, then this
corruption would be intensified in proportion to
the degree in which the original revelation was
overlaid.[1] In the Hellenic mythology this pro-

[1] The same argument seems to be of force against the supposition that a revelation so extensive as that assumed by Mr.
Gladstone preceded the age whose language gave birth to the
later Aryan mythology. For a revelation so corrupted implies a
gradual degeneration into coarseness, sensuality, and even brutishness: but the mind of that early time, as exhibited to us in
their language, is childish or infantile, but not brutish; and it is
not easy to see how from a period in which they had sensualised
and debased a high revelation, men could emerge into a state of
simple and childish wonder, altogether distinct whether from
idolatry or impurity, and in which their notions as to the life

cess is reversed. Even as it appears in the Homeric poems, it must have undergone a development of centuries; but if it is impossible to measure, by any reference to an older Greek literature, the personality and attributes of each god as compared with the conceptions of a previous age, it is obvious that the general tone of feeling and action, and the popular standard of morality, had not been debased with the growth of their mythology. The Hesiodic poems belong confessedly to a later time than the epics of Homer; but if their theology is more systematised, and their theogony more repulsive, their morality and philosophy is immeasurably higher and more true. The latter may not exhibit the same heroic strength, they may betray a querulous spirit not unlike that of the Jewish Preacher; but they display a conviction of the perfect justice and equity of the Divine Being, and an appreciation of goodness, as being equally the duty and the interest of mankind [1], which we could scarcely de-

of nature were as indefinite and unformed as their ideas respecting their own personality.

[1] See especially the striking analogy of the broad and narrow ways leading respectively to ruin and happiness. (Works and Days, 285—290.) It is not pretended that this morality, many of the precepts of which seem almost echoes from the Sermon on the Mount, was handed down from an original revelation. If then in this respect the course was from the lesser to the greater, the progress could be the work only of the Spirit of

sire to have strengthened.¹ With the growth of a mythology and its more systematic arrangement, the perception of moral truth has become more keen and intense; and the same age which listened to the generations of Zeus, Kronos, and Alphroditê, learnt wisdom from the pensive precepts of the 'Works and Days.'

It is perhaps difficult to determine how far the characters of Phœbus and Athênê have been drawn out and systematised by the genius and moral instinct of the poet himself. We have no evidence, in any extant literature, of the precise state in which he found the national mythology; but it is hard to think that he had what may be termed a theological authority for every statement which he makes and every attribute which he assigns to the one or the other. It is certain that Athênê once conspired against the freedom of Zeus²; but we cannot tell how far the poet himself intensified the general

Comparison of the Homeric with the Vedic mythology.

God; and the downward course of their mythology from a positive revelation appears therefore the more mysterious and perplexing.

¹ The 'Works and Days' of Hesiod seem to exhibit, along with some decline of physical energy, a sensitiveness of temperament to which the idea of overbearing arrogance and wanton insult threw a dark colouring over the whole course of human life. With such a feeling the mind may easily pass into a morbid condition.

² Iliad, i. 400.

harmony of her will to that of the king of gods and men. But language has furnished an evidence, which it is impossible to resist, of the gradual process which imparted to these mythical deities both their personality and their attributes. The literature of another branch of the same Aryan race exhibits a mythology whose identity with that of the Greeks it is impossible to dispute; but in that mythology beings, whose personality in the Homeric poems is sharply drawn, and whose attributes are strictly defined, are still dim and shadowy. Even the great Olympian king has not received the passions and appetites, and certainly not the form of man.* Nay, in that older mythology their persons and their attributes are alike interchangeable. That which among the Greeks we find as a highly developed and complicated system is elsewhere a mere mass of floating legend, nay, almost of mere mythical phrases, without plan or cohesion. This difference, at first sight so perplexing, may itself enable us to discover the great secret of the origin and growth of all mythology; but the fact remains indisputable, that in the Vedas, to use the words of Professor Max Müller, 'the whole nature of these so-called gods is still transparent, their first conception in many cases clearly perceptible. There are as yet no genealogies, no settled marriages between gods and goddesses. The father is sometimes the son, the brother is the husband, and she who in one hymn is the mother is in another the wife. As the conceptions of the poet vary, so varies the nature of these gods. Nowhere is the wide distance which separates the ancient poems of India from the most ancient literature of Greece more clearly felt than when we compare the growing myths of the Veda with the full-grown and decayed myths on which the poetry of Homer is founded.'[1] But the unformed mythology of the Vedas followed in its own land a course analogous to that of the mythology of Greece. There was the same systematic development, with this difference, that in India the process was urged on by a powerful sacerdotal order who found their interest in the expansion of the old belief. In the earlier Vedas there is no predominant priesthood, and only the faintest indications of caste; there are no temples or public worship, and, as it would seem, no images of the gods; but, what is of immeasurably greater importance in reference to the mythological creed of Homer, there are, as Professor Wilson has observed, 'no indications of a triad, the creating, preserving, and destroying power. Brahma does not appear as a deity, and Vishnu, although

[1] Essay on Comparative Mythology, in Oxford Essays for 1856, p. 47.

named, has nothing in common with the Vishnu of the Puranas; no allusion occurs to his Avataras. . . . These differences are palpable, and so far from the Vedas being the basis of the existing system, they completely overturn it.'[1] The comparison is scarcely less fatal to the mythological Trinity of Homer.

We come at length to the question of fact. What was the measure of divine truth imparted to man Methods of determining the extent of primitive revelation. on his creation or immediately after the fall, and under what forms was it conveyed? And if, when stated thus, the question should be one which we cannot absolutely determine, we may yet ask, was it a revelation as explicit and extensive as Mr. Gladstone represents it to have been? To allege the rabbinical traditions and speculations of comparatively recent times [2] as evidence for the latent meaning of Greek mythology, is to treat the subject in a way which would simply make any solution of the problem impossible. The force of a current, when its stream has been divided, will not tell us much about the course or the depth of

---

[1] Professor H. H. Wilson, in Edinburgh Review for October 1860, No. ccxxviii. p. 382. His remarks on the general character of the Vedic religion deserve the deepest attention. They seem entirely to subvert the hypothesis which Mr. Gladstone has so ably maintained.

[2] Gladstone, Homer, &c. vol. ii. p. 50.

kindred streams which have branched off in other directions. And, accordingly, although later traditions appear to be blended in his idea of the primitive belief [1], yet Mr. Gladstone rightly insists that the Homeric theology must, if his hypothesis be correct, show the vestiges of a traditional knowledge, 'derived from the epoch when the covenant of God with man and the promise of a Messiah had not yet fallen within the contracted forms of Judaism for shelter,' [2] and that these traditions must 'carry upon them the mark of belonging to the religion which the Book of Genesis represents as brought by our first parents from Paradise and as delivered by them to their immediate descendants in general.' [3] Thus the era of the division of races is the latest limit to which we can bring down a common tradition for all mankind; and for that tradition we are confined to the first eleven chapters of the Book of Genesis.

From these chapters we must derive our proof that our first parents and their immediate descendants possessed the idea of an Infinite Being whose perfect goodness arose not from external restraints, but from an unchangeable internal determination of character [4], — of a Trinity of Coequal Persons in the Divine

Evidence of the Book of Genesis.

[1] Gladstone, Homer, &c. vol. ii. p. 46.
[2] Ibid. p. 3.   [3] Ibid. p. 4.   [4] Ibid. p. 18.

Unity,—of a Redeemer who should hereafter assume their nature and deliver from death and sin,—of a Divine Wisdom which was with God from the beginning, and of an Evil One who, having fallen from his throne in heaven, had now become an antagonistic power, tempting men to their destruction.[1]

Its character.
Whether these early chapters may contain this theological scheme by just and legitimate inference, whether the words there written may contain the earnest and the warrant of the full Christian revelation, are questions with which we are not here concerned. It is not a question of doctrine or belief or theological analysis. It is a simple question of fact which must determine whether various races of mankind were, or not, guilty of wilful perversion of high and mysterious doctrines. Here, if anywhere, that purification of the intellect would seem to be needed, the lack of which substitutes traditional teaching or association for an impartial sifting of evidence.[2] There was a time when these early records formed the whole literature of the people; and, to adopt Mr. Gladstone's ex-

---

[1] Gladstone, Homer, &c. vol. ii. p. 42.
[2] The necessity of such a process in all questions of fact will scarcely be disputed; and the present would seem strictly to fall under this class. See Grote, History of Greece, vol. viii. pp. 617—620.

pression, it would not be 'safe to make any large assumption respecting a traditional knowledge of any parts of early revelation,' beyond what those records actually contain.[1] Taken wholly by themselves, and not interpreted by the light thrown on them by the thought and belief of later ages, these records tell us of man as being (in some sense not explicitly defined) made in the Divine image and likeness,—of one positive prohibition, the violation of which was to be followed by immediate death,—of a subtle beast which tempts the woman to disobey the command, and of a sense of shame which follows the transgression. They tell us of flight from the Divine presence when the man hears the voice of God walking in the garden in the cool of the day,—of an attempt to transfer the blame from the man to the woman, from the woman to the serpent,—of a sentence of humiliation passed upon the latter, with the warning that its head should be bruised by the woman's seed,—of a life of toil and labour for the former, ending with a return to the dust from which he had been made. And besides this, they tell us briefly that after some generations men began to call upon the name of the Lord; that in course of time they sank (with but one exception) into brute lust and violence; and

[1] Gladstone, Homer, &c. vol. ii. p. 40.

that, on the renovation of the earth, men were made answerable for each other's blood, and received the token of the rainbow as a warrant for the future permanence of the course of nature.

If the doctrines which, in Mr. Gladstone's belief, made up the primitive revelation, are contained in these chapters, it is, as he admits, by a dim and feeble foreshadowing.[1] They tell us nothing of God in the perfection of His nature, or of a unity of Three Persons in the Godhead. They tell us of a subtle serpent, not of a fallen angel, of the seed of the woman as bruising that serpent's head, not of a Divine Redeemer delivering from sin and spiritual death. Still less do they tell us of a Divine Wisdom, of an institution of sacrifice[2], or of a spiritual communion in prayer as existing from the first between man and God. All these doctrines may be legitimate deductions; but if to us the record itself gives only mysterious glimpses of a future fuller revelation, if to us these inferences from its contents are the result of careful comparison with the later

Limits of that evidence.

---

[1] Gladstone, Homer, &c. vol. ii. p. 39.
[2] The fact of offerings is obviously very different from an ordinance commanding such offerings. The former may exist without the latter. Nor is there the slightest intimation that the offering of Cain was rejected because it was not one of blood: its rejection is made to depend not on the quality of the oblation but on the moral condition of him who brings it.

books of the Old Testament, if even to us their harmony with the belief of prophets and righteous men of later ages is clear because we have been taught to see that it is clear, then what evidence have we that in the time, of which the third chapter of Genesis speaks to us, our first parents had a full apprehension of what to us is faint and shadowy? For if on the revelation made to them the vast mass of Greek mythology grew up as a corrupt incrustation, they must have received these truths not in their germ, but in full dogmatic statement. It is difficult to understand how such a statement could have been to them anything more than a dead formula, waiting to be quickened into life by the breath of a later revelation.

If again there is any one lesson which may be drawn before others from the character of the early records in the Old Testament, it is that ideas, dim and feeble at first, acquire gradually strength and consistency, that the clearness of revelation is heightened as its stream widens, and that all positive belief is the result of years and generations of discipline. But in some mysterious way, while the course of the Jewish people was from the lesser to the greater, they in whose hands the theology of Homer was moulded, started with a fulness of doctrinal knowledge which was not attained by

<small>Course of revelation in the Old Testament.</small>

the former until a long series of centuries had passed away.

And if a hearty acceptance of the records of the Book of Genesis involves no assumption of the pre-vious existence of traditions or doctrines not mentioned in those records, it frees us not less from the necessity of supposing that in all but the Jewish world a process was going on which presents, to say the least, a hard trial for our faith. But while we assent to Mr. Gladstone's remark on the ease with which these foreshadowings of the Trinity and of Redemption might pass into polytheism and anthropomorphism[1], it would scarcely argue a spirit of irreverence if we asked why they should receive doctrinal statements which they could not understand, and which, under these conditions, rendered such a transition not merely probable, but inevitable?

Greek corruption of revelation.

There is an instinctive reluctance to accept any theory which heightens human depravity and corruption, unless there are weighty reasons for doing so. And unquestionably, on the hypothesis which has just been examined, the mythology of the Greeks exhibits an instance of wilful and profane perversion, to which perhaps we can find no parallel. But the character of that mythology still remains, when

Necessity of accounting for the character of Greek mythology.

---
[1] Gladstone, Homer, vol. ii. p. 43.

we have rejected this supposition. We have still before us the chronicles or legends of gods who not merely eat and drink and sleep, but display the working of the vilest of human passions. Some process, therefore, either conscious or unconscious, must have brought about a result so perplexing. And if even for conscious invention there must have been some groundwork, much more must this be the case if we take up an alternative which even less admits the exercise of a creative faculty.

If examined without reference to the revelation or tradition of later ages, the earlier records of the Book of Genesis itself may help us in some measure to solve the mystery. We cannot argue from the silence of those opening chapters, with more safety than from the silence of Homer. Of the length of time which elapsed before the fall we are ignorant, and therefore we cannot tell whether it was long enough to leave any permanent impression on the mind [1];

Actual statements of the Book of Genesis.

---

[1] In the absence of any explicit statement of time, there is nothing to warrant the supposition that the temptation was long or often repeated. It would seem from the narrative that the command to abstain from the forbidden fruit was followed immediately by the serpent's suggestion, on which the woman acted as soon as she saw that the tree was good for food. The mental process which determined this might be long, but it might also be very short. The narrative in Genesis does not imply any such extended life in the garden as would at all

and for the period after the fall we have the expression of a sense of shame, of the consciousness of guilt, and of sentence passed on the transgressor. This alone would amount to a revelation; nor can we refuse that name even to the first feeble glimmer of mind and spirit as roused into activity by the consciousness of existence. But of the sensations produced and the thoughts awakened in them by the objects and phenomena of the outward world we have no record whatever; and it is scarcely safe to fall back on the analogy of infancy and childhood, as these might be if severed from all associations of later thought and knowledge.

It is almost impossible to avoid the conclusion that the consciousness of his own existence would lead man to attribute the same life to every single thing on which his eyes might rest. Of all those objects he had no positive knowledge, whether of their origin, their nature, or their properties. But he had life, and therefore all things else must have life also. He was under no necessity of personifying them, for he had for himself no distinctions between consciousness and personality. He knew nothing

<small>Earliest condition of thought and its consequences.</small>

---

suffice for the varied events introduced by Milton into his 'Paradise Lost.' His chronology springs from the same imagination which invested Satan with more than the colossal proportions of Geryon and Briareos.

of the conditions of his own life or of any other, and therefore all things on the earth or in the heavens were invested with the same vague idea of existence. The sun, the moon, the stars, the ground on which he trod, the clouds and storms and lightnings, were all living beings: could he help thinking that, like himself, they were conscious beings also? His very words would by an inevitable necessity express this conviction. His language would admit no single expression from which the attribute of life was excluded, while it would vary the forms of that life with an almost inexhaustible variety. Every object would be a living reality, and every word a speaking picture. For him there would be no bare recurrence of days and seasons, but each morning the dawn would drive her bright flocks to the blue pastures of heaven, before the birth of the lord of day from the toiling womb of night. Round the living progress of the new-born sun there would be grouped a lavish imagery, expressive of the most intense sympathy with what we term the operation of material forces, and not less expressive of the utter absence of even the faintest knowledge. Life would be an alternation of joy and sorrow, of terror and relief; for every evening the dawn would return leading her bright flocks, and the short-lived sun would die. Years might pass, or ages, before his rising again would establish even the weakest analogy; but in the meanwhile they would mourn for his death as for the loss of one who might never return.[1] For every aspect of the material world he would have ready some life-giving expression; and those aspects would be scarcely less varied than his words. The same object would at different times or under different conditions awaken the most opposite or inconsistent conceptions. But these conceptions and the words which expressed them would exist side by side without the slightest consciousness of their incongruity; nor is it easy to determine the exact order in which they might arise. The sun would awaken both mournful and inspiriting ideas,—ideas of victory and defeat, of toil and premature death. He would be the Titan, strangling the serpents of the night before he drove his chariot up the sky; and he would also be the being who, worn down by unwilling labour undergone for men, sinks wearied into the arms of the mother who bare him in the morning. Other images would not be wanting; the dawn and the dew and the violet clouds of morning would be not less real and living than the sun. In his rising

[1] This state of thought is most forcibly brought out by Professor Müller, Comparative Mythology, in Oxford Essays for 1856, p. 59. As contrasted with this mental condition, our forms of expression may well be said to exhibit a 'Titanic assurance.'

from the east he would quit the fair Iolê whom he should see no more till his labour drew towards its close. And not less would he love and be loved by the dew and by the morning herself, while to both his love would be fatal as his fiery car rose higher in the sky. So would man speak of all other things also, of the thunder and the earthquake and the storm, not less than of summer and winter. But it would be no personification, and still less would it be an allegory or a metaphor. It would be to him a veritable reality, which he examined and analysed as little as he reflected on himself. It would be a sentiment and a belief, but in no sense a religion.

It is obvious that such a form of thought and expression would accommodate itself to any place and every climate; it would have as much room for its exercise in the frozen mountains of the North as under the most smiling sky and genial sun. But it would also be a period of transition, in which the idea of existence would be sooner or later expanded into that of personality. But probably before this change had taken place, the yet unbroken family of mankind would be scattered to seek new homes in distant lands; and the gradual change of language, which that dispersion rendered inevitable, would involve a more momentous change in their belief. They would carry away with

This condition was one of transition.

them the old words and expressions; but these would now be associated with new ideas, or else be imperfectly or wrongly understood. Henceforth the sun and moon would not merely be living things, but living persons, while the morning and evening, failing perhaps to reach this personality, would leave behind them a number of phrases from which would spring a goodly harvest of fable and legend. From personification to deification the steps would be very rapid; and the process of disintegration would at once furnish the materials for a vast fabric of mythology. All the expressions which had attached a living force to natural objects would remain as the description of personal and anthropomorphous gods. Every word would become an attribute, and all ideas once grouped round a single object would branch off into distinct personifications. The sun had been the lord of light, the driver of the chariot of the day, he had toiled and laboured for the sons of men, and sunk down to rest, after hard battle, in the evening. But now the lord of light would be Phœbus Apollo, while Helios would remain enthroned in his fiery chariot, and his toils and labours and death-struggles would be transferred to Heracles. The violet clouds which greet his rising and his setting would now be represented by the maiden Iolê or by herds of cows which feed in earthly pastures.

There would be other expressions which would still remain as floating phrases, not attached to any definite deities. These would gradually be converted into incidents in the life of heroes, and be woven at length into systematic narrative. Finally these gods or heroes, and the incidents of their mythical career, would receive each 'a local habitation and a name.' These would remain as genuine history, when the origin and meaning of the words had been either wholly or in part forgotten.

But in such a process as this it is manifest that the men amongst whom it sprang up would not be responsible for the form which it might assume. Words, applied at first simply to outward objects or phenomena, would become the names of personal gods; and the phrases which described those objects would then be transferred to what were now deities to be adored. But it would not follow that a form of thought, which might apply not only without harm but with a marvellous beauty to things if living yet not personal, would bear translation into the conditions of human life. If in the older speech the heaven was wedded to the earth which returned his love with a prodigal fertility, in the later time the name of the heaven would be the name of a god, and that god would necessarily be earthly and sensual. But this develop-

Development of Greek mythology.

ment of a mythology, much of which would inevitably be immoral and even repulsive, would not necessarily exercise a similar debasing influence on the morality and practice of the people. It had started with being a sentiment, not a religion,—a personal conviction, but not a moral belief; and the real Object of the heart's adoration would remain not less distinct from the creations of mythology than it had been before. Nay, it might be that with any given people the tone of thought and the character of society might be more and more raised, even while the incongruous mythological fabric assumed more stupendous proportions. But the first condition of thought, which regarded every object in creation as endowed with life, could have *in itself* only two possible developments. It must issue either in an anthropomorphous polytheism, or a degrading fetiche worship.[1] The character of the people would in each case determine whether the result for them should be an idolatrous terror of inanimate things, or the multiplication of deities with human forms and human passions, mingling with men and sharing their partialities and their feuds.

For the proof of these assertions we shall look

[1] In the growth of a higher belief and a purer morality by the side and in spite of the popular mythology, we can see only the operation of the Divine Spirit on the mind and heart of men.

in vain to the earliest Hellenic literature; but the Vedic poems furnish indisputable evidence that such as this was the origin and growth of Greek mythology. In these poems the names of many, perhaps of most of the Greek gods, indicate natural objects which, if endued with life, have not been reduced to human personality. In them Daphnê is still simply the morning twilight ushering in the splendour of the new-born sun; the cattle of Helios there are still the light clouds whom the dawn (Eôs) leads out into the fields of the sky. There the idea of Heracles has not yet been separated from the image of the toiling and struggling sun, and the splendour of the life-giving Helios has not been transferred to the god of Delos and Pytho. In the Vedas the myths of Endymion, of Kephalos and Prokris, Orpheus and Eurydikê, are exhibited under the detached mythical phrases which furnished for each their germ.[1] The analysis may be extended indefinitely; but the conclusion can only show that in the Vedic language we have the foundation not only of the glowing legends of Hellas, but of the dark and sombre mythology of the Scandinavian and the Teuton. Both alike have grown up chiefly from names which have been

(marginal note: Evidence for this development furnished by the Vedas.)

[1] All these legends, with others, are minutely analysed by Professor Max Müller, Comparative Mythology, pp. 50—87.

grouped around the sun; but the former has been grounded on those expressions which describe the recurrence of day and night, the latter on the great tragedy of nature in the alternation of summer and winter.

Of this vast mass of solar myths some have emerged into independent legends, others have furnished the groundwork of whole epics, others have remained simply as floating tales, whose intrinsic beauty no poet has wedded to his verse. Whether the whole may be classified in order of priority, may perhaps be doubtful; but the strong presumption would be that those which have not been systematised into coherent narratives are the oldest. At the least they exhibit to us the substance of mythology in its earliest form. Thus the legends of Kephalos and Prokris, of Daphnê, and of Endymion, have come down to us in a less artificial form than that of Herakles; while that of Herakles has been arrested at a less advanced stage than those of Zeus and Apollo. But all alike can be translated back into mythical expressions, and most of these expressions are found in the Vedas with their strict mythical meaning. The marvellous exuberance of this early language, and the wealth of its synonyms[1], may well excite

[margin note: Relative age of Greek myths.]

---

[1] For the results of this *Polyonymy* and *Synonymy*, see Max Müller, Comparative Mythology, p. 44, &c.

astonishment, as we watch its divergence into such myths as those of Kephalos and Endymion, Herakles, Daphnê, the Pythian and Delian Apollo, Phaethon and Meleagros, Memnon and Bellerophon.

All these tell us of the sun under some of the many aspects which suggested each their own mythical expression. When the language of mythology was the ordinary speech of daily life, the Night laboured and heaved with the birth of the coming Day. There was for her no rest until the time came when he should spring up again in the freshness of renewed youth. This toil and labour is reproduced in the Homeric hymn; and Lêto, the power of forgetfulness and sleep, gives birth to the lord of light in Delos [1] (III.). His coming is preceded by the pale Twilight, who, in mythical times, drove his cows to their pastures; but in the Odyssey his herds feed at Tænaron or in Thrinakia far away, where Phaethusa and Lampetiê, the bright and gleaming children of Neaira, the early morn, tend them at the rising and setting of the sun (XXVIIL).

Solar myths.

---

[1] The localising of Phœbus at Delos or in Lykia arose from the fact that the meaning of the two names, as expressive of *Light*, had been forgotten. So Endymion is localised in the cave of Latmos, a word which has the same origin with Léthê, and the Latin *lethum* (death), and Lêtô (or the night), the mother of Phœbus himself.

The old mythical feeling is strikingly manifest throughout the whole legend, not merely in the names and office of the wife and children of Helios, but in the delight with which he gazes on his cattle at the beginning and the close of his daily course, and in the indignation which prompts him to hide his light in the regions of the dead. But the sun loves not only the Clouds; he loves the fair Dawn who is their leader; and so the Dawn comes before us as followed by him and flying from his love, or else as returning it. The former mythical phrase ('the dawn flies from the sun') is embodied in the legend of Daphnê, who flies from her lover and vanishes away as he seeks to embrace her (II.). In the tale of Orpheus[1], she appears, under the name of Eurydikê, as the bride of the sun, loved by him and returning his love, and yet falling a victim to it, for whether to Daphnê or Eurydikê the brightness of his glance is fatal as he rises higher in the heaven. The same feeling is manifest, under a form if possible more intense, in the tale of Kephalos and Procris (I.). 'The sun loves the dew' was the old mythical phrase; and it is reproduced in the love of Kephalos[2] (the head of the sun) for Procris (the glittering dewdrop). But the 'Morning loves the sun.' Eôs seeks to

---

[1] See Tales from Greek Mythology, p. 17.
[2] See Max Müller, Comparative Mythology, p. 63.

win Kephalos for herself; and her jealousy of Procris is at once explained. Yet again the dewdrops each reflect the sun, and Procris becomes faithless to her lover, while she grants him her love under a new disguise; and finally, when her fault has been atoned, she dies by the spear of Artemis (the fiery ray), with which the sun unwittingly strikes her down. It is the old tale of Daphnê and Eurydikê; and Kephalos goes mourning on his solitary journey, labouring not for himself but for men who need his help[1], until he sinks to sleep beneath the western sea.

Again, throughout his daily course, the action of the sun is various. If his light is beneficent, his heat is often destructive; or dark clouds from time to time hide his splendours. Sometimes he toils for the good of men, sometimes he slays them. Sometimes he sinks to his rest in quietness and peace, while the Moon comes to give him her greeting of love; sometimes he dies after a battle with the struggling clouds, leaving a solitary line of blood-red light behind him. So in the Hellenic legend—Phœbus cannot rest in his bright birthplace of Lykia or Delos; he must wander far westwards over many lands, through the fair vale of Telphûsa, to his

Changeful action of the sun.

[1] In this legend, he goes to the aid of Amphitryon; but such details might, of course, be varied at will.

western home in Delphi (IV.). There the mighty power of his rays is shown in the death of the great dragon[1], whose body is left to rot at Pytho. Yet it was strange that the sun, whose influence was commonly for life and gladness, should sometimes vex and slay the sons of men; and so the tale went that plague and pestilence came when Phaethon had taken the place of Helios and sought in vain to guide aright his fire-breathing horses (VIII.). So again the legend of Meleagros exhibits only the capricious action of the sun, and the alternations of light and shade are expressed in the sudden exploits and moody sullenness of the hero (VII.); but his life is bound up with the torch of Day, the burning brand; and when its last spark flickers out, the life of the hero is ended. More commonly, however, he is the mighty one labouring on and finally worn out by an unselfish toil, struggling in his hard task for a being who is not worthy of the great and costly sacrifice. So Phœbus Apollo, with his kinsman Heracles, serves the Trojan Laomedon (XXIV.); and so he dwells as a bondsman in the house of Admetos. So likewise, as Bellerophon, he encounters fearful peril at the bidding of a treacherous host (XXI.), and dies,

---

[1] We have here only a reproduction of the snakes which are killed by Heracles, and the serpent which stings Eurydikê. It reappears in Norse mythology as the serpent Fafnir.

like Sarpedon and Memnon (xxv.), in a quarrel which is not his own. But nowhere is his unutterable toil and scanty reward brought out so prominently as in the whole legend, or rather the mass of unconnected legend, which is gathered round the person of Herakles.[1] Doomed before his birth (vi.) to be the slave of a weak and cruel master, while yet in his cradle, he strangles the serpents of the night, the same serpents which stung to death the fair Eurydikê. His toils begin. His limbs are endued with an irresistible power, and he has a soul which knows no fear. He may use this power for good or for evil; and his choice for good furnishes the groundwork for the fable of Prodicos. Other legends there were which perverted this idea; and in these he is exhibited under gross uncouth or repulsive forms.[2] But he goes upon his way, and very early in his course he sees and loves the maiden Iolê.[3] With her he would dwell; but

[1] The collection and systematic arrangement of his labours was the work of a much later age than that of Homer.

[2] See Grote (History of Greece, vol. i. p. 129), for the comic character which came to be attached to Herakles. The Alcestis of Euripides is an instance which at once suggests itself.

[3] With this name may possibly be connected the myth of the poison (*iós*) which makes the arrows of Philoctetes and the robes of Deianeira and Medeia fatal. The name certainly points to the violet-coloured clouds which float in the sky at sunrise and sunset.

his doom gives him no rest, and he is hurried away through many lands. In all he has mighty works to do, and he fails in none. The remembrance of the fair maiden may linger in his memory, but there are others who claim his love in the days of his strength and power, and it would seem as though he had forgotten the daughter of Eurytos. But his time draws towards its close; the beautiful maiden, whose face had gladdened him as he was setting out upon his toil, returns to cheer him in the evening of his life. With her comes the poisoned robe (the battle of the darkening clouds), which he strives in vain to tear away from his bleeding limbs. In a deeper and redder stream flows the lifeblood, till, after a convulsive struggle, the strife is closed in the dead silence of night.

But it is in the case of Heracles that the perfect truth of the old mythical language gave rise more especially to that apparently strange and perplexing meaning which repelled and disgusted even the poets and philosophers of Greece. Pindar utterly refuses to believe that any god could be a glutton or a sensualist; he might in the same spirit have rejected the tales which impute something of meanness or cowardice to the brave and highsouled Heracles. For Heracles fights with poi-

Repulsive developments of solar legends.

soned arrows[1], and leaves them as his bequest to Philoctetes. But the poisoned arrows are the piercing rays which burn in the tropical noonday, and they reappear as well in the poisoned robe of Deianeira as in that which the Colchian Medeia professes to have received from her kinsman Helios (XIX.).

A deeper mythical meaning, however, underlies and accounts for the immorality and licence which was introduced into the transmuted legend of Heracles. The sun looks down on the earth; and the earth answers to his loving glance by her teeming and inexhaustible fertility. In every land she yields her special harvest, of fruits and flowers, of corn and wine and oil. Her children are countless; but all spring up under the eye of the sun as he journeys through the wide heaven. It is easy to see what must be the result when the sun is transmuted into the human yet godlike Heracles, and how repulsive that myth must become which in its primitive form only sang how—

<blockquote>
'The sunlight clasps the earth,
And the moonbeams kiss the sea.'[2].
</blockquote>

Origin of these developments.

The same explanation removes the mystery of the

---

[1] At the least, the arrows which are his bequest to Philoctetes are steeped in deadly poison. They give Paris his death-wound. See Œnonè (XXVI.)

[2] Shelley, Love's Philosophy.

even greater degradation to which the Hellenic mythology reduced Zeus himself, the supreme father of gods and men. He who ought to be the type of all purity and goodness is the very embodiment of headstrong lust and passion, while the holiness of the lord of life and light is transferred to Apollo and his virgin sister Athênê. The difficulty is but slight. Zeus (the Sanskrit Dyaus) is but another form of Ouranos, the heaven or sky [1]; and again, as in the words of our own poet, who sings how—

> 'Nothing in the world is single,
> All things by a law divine
> In another's being mingle,'

and how—

> 'The mountains kiss high heaven,'

so Ouranos looked down on Gaia (or Demeter), and brooded over her in his deep, unfailing, life-giving love. But these are phrases which will not bear translation into the conditions of human life without degrading the spiritual god into a being who boasts of his unbounded and shameless licence.

---

[1] In the language of Hesiod, Uranos covers everything; and in Sanskrit Varuna, from the root *var*, to cover, is a name of the firmament. (Max Müller, Comparative Mythology, p. 41.) So again, in Sanskrit, Dyaus (Zeus) is the sky; and the attributes of Ouranos could at once be transferred to Zeus, and would be developed into a mass of erotic legend.

The same process which insured this degradation insured at the same time the local boundaries which were assigned to mythical heroes or their mythical exploits. When the adventures of Zeus assumed something like consistency, the original meaning of his name was less and less remembered, until his birthplace was fixed in the Dictæan cave, and his throne raised on Olympus. So Apollo was born in Lykia or in Delos, and dwelt at Patara or Pytho. So Endymion had his tomb in Elis, or slept his long sleep on the hill of Latmos. So Kephalos first met Procris on the Hymettian heights, and fell from the Leucadian cape into the western sea. So, as she wandered westwards in search of her lost child, Telephassa [1] sank to sleep on the Thessalian plain in the evening.

Tendency to localise mythical incidents.

Yet, although much was forgotten, and much also, it may be, lost for ever, the form of thought which produced the old mythical language had not altogether died away. Showing itself sometimes in directly allegorical statement of historical fact, sometimes in similar descriptions of natural objects or the incidents of common life, it still threw the halo of a living reality over everything of which it spoke. So the flight of Kaunos from Miletus to Lykia, and

Vitality of the mythopœic faculty.

[1] The name (like those of Phaethûsa, Lampetié, and Brenhyldr) tells its own tale.

the sorrow of the sister whom he had left behind, figured the migration of colonists from the one land to the other.¹ So in the Hesiodic Theogony, Night is the mother of Hupnos (sleep) and Oneiros (dream), of Eris (strife) and Apatê (deceit) and Mômos (blame), where we speak merely of sleeping and dreaming and of evil deeds wrought in secresy and darkness.²

If again the mythology of Homer, as handed down to us, points to an age long anterior to his own, yet the mythopœic faculty still exerted itself, if not in the invention of myths altogether new, yet in the embellishment and the expansion of the old. It was not easy to satisfy the appetite of an imaginative age which had no canon of historical criticism, and which constantly craved its fitting food. It was not easy to exhaust the vein opened up in almost every mythical theme. The sun as toiling and suffering — the sky as brooding over and cherishing the earth — the light as gladdening and purifying all visible things, would suggest an infinity of details illustrating each original idea. The multiplication of miracles and marvels simply stimulated the desire for more;

<small>Constant demand for new mythical narratives.</small>

---

¹ See Max Müller (Comparative Mythology, p. 42) for many similar instances.
² Ibid. p. 40.

and new labours were invented for Heracles, new loves for Zeus, as easily as their forefathers uttered the words to which the myths of Zeus and Heracles owed their existence. The mere fact of their human personification insured the growth of innumerable fictions. If Zeus had the form and the passions of men, then the conditions of his life must be assimilated to theirs. He must have wife and children, he must have father and mother. The latter must be no less divine than himself; but as he is enthroned above them, they must belong to a dynasty which he has overthrown. Their defeat must have been preceded by a long and fierce struggle. Mighty beings of gigantic force must have fought on each side in that tremendous conflict; but the victory must belong to the side which to brute force added wise forethought and prudent counsel.[1] Here, then, would be the foundation for that marvellous supernatural machinery of which we have some indications in the Iliad, and which is drawn out with such careful detail in the Hesiodic Theogony. But Zeus, to whom there were children born in every land, must have his queen; and the jealousy of Hêrê against Iô or Semelê or Alcmenê would follow as a necessary consequence. The subject might be indefinitely expanded, and

[1] Hence the mythical Prometheus.

each subject would of itself suggest others; but there was no fear that the poet should weary the patience of his hearers, if only his additions, whether of incident or detail, did not violate the law of mythological credibility. Nothing must be related of Heracles which was repugnant to the fundamental idea of his toil and suffering for a master weaker than himself; nothing must be told of Athênê which would rather call up associations of the laughter-loving Aphroditê.

And, finally, there would be a constant and irresistible temptation to sever historical inci-

Transmutation of names really historical.

dents and characters from the world of reality and bear them into the cloudland of mythology. Round every hero who after great promise died in the spring-time of his life, or on whom the yoke of an unworthy tyrant lay heavy, would be grouped words and expressions which belonged to the myth of the brilliant yet quickly dying sun. The tale of Achilles and Meleagros may be entirely mythical; but even if it be in part the story of men who really lived and suffered, that story has been interwoven with images borrowed from the myths of a bygone age. Nay, the occurrence of such a name as Meleagros is no warrant that the version of an earlier day may not have given him a name more in accordance with the mythical idea. Names unquestionably historical have been introduced into the Nibelungen Lied, which are not to be found in the Edda. The great Theodoric at Verona is transmuted into Dietrich von Bern, while Siegbert, the Austrasian king, and the infamous Brunehault [1], have taken the place of Sigurdr, in whose wife Brenhyldr we recognise the beautiful Lampetiê of the Odyssey. But if the mythical phrases which gave birth to the legends of Heracles, Endymion, and Orpheus, of Phaethon, Meleagros, and Bellerophon, spoke of the daily course of the sun, there were others which told of alternating seasons. For this mythical speech could adapt itself to every land and climate; and its character would be modified, and its very phrases suggested, by the outward features and phenomena of the country. The speech of the

Groundwork of the mythology of Northern Europe.

[1] In this instance the 'coincidence between myth and history is so great that it has induced some Euhemeristic critics to derive the whole legend of the *Nibelunge* from Austrasian history, and to make the murder of Siegbert by Brunehault the basis of the murder of Sifrit or Sigurdr by Brenhyldr. Fortunately, it is easier to answer these German than the old Greek Euhemerists; for we find in contemporary history that Jornandes, who wrote his history at least twenty years before the death of the Austrasian Siegbert, knew already the daughter of the mythic Sigurdr, Swanhild, who was born, 'according to the Edda, after the murder of his father, and afterwards killed by Jormunrekr, whom the poem has again historicised in Hermanicus, a Gothic king of the fourth century.'—*Max Müller, Comparative Mythology*, p. 68.

tropics, and still more of the happy zone which lies beyond its scorching heat, would tell rather of brilliance than of gloom, of life rather than decay, of constant renovation rather than prolonged lethargy. But in the frost-bound regions of the North the speech of the people would, with a peculiar intensity of feeling, dwell on the tragedy of Nature. It would speak not so much of the daily death of the sun, for the recurrence of day and night in other lands would bring no darkness to these; but of the deadly sleep of the earth, when the powers of frost and snow had vanquished the brilliant king. It would speak not of Eôs rising from the Titan's couch, or of Hêlios sinking wearied into his golden cup beyond the sea; but of treasures stolen from the earth and buried in her hidden depths beyond the sight and reach of man. It would tell of a fair maiden wrapped in a dreamless slumber from which the touch of one brave knight alone could rouse her; it would sing of her rescue, her betrothal, and her desertion, as the sun who brought back the spring forsook her for the gay and wanton summer. It would go on to frame tales of strife and jealousy ending in the death of the bright hero; it would speak of the wife whom he has forsaken, as going up to die upon his funeral pile. This woful tragedy, whose long sorrow called forth a deep and intense sympathy which we, perhaps, can scarcely realise, is faintly indicated in the beautiful hymn to Dêmêtêr [1]; but winter in the bright Hellenic land assumed a form too fair to leave any deep impression of gloom and death on the popular mythology. The face of nature suggested there the simple tale which speaks of Persephonê as stolen away, but brought back to her mother by a covenant insuring to her a longer sojourn on the bright earth than in the shadowy kingdom of Hades. But how completely the tragedy, to which this hymn points, forms the groundwork of the Volsung Tale and of the Edda into which it was expanded, to what an extent it has suggested the most minute details of the great epics of the North, Professor Max Müller has shown with a force and clearness which leaves no room for doubt.[2] Like Achilles, Sifrit or

[1] Tales from Greek Mythology, vol. i. p. 98, &c.

[2] Comparative Mythology, p. 66, &c. The story of Sigurdr and Brenhyldr comes up again in the legends of Ragnar and Thora, and again of Ragnar and Aslauga. Like Brenhyldr, Thora with the earth's treasure is guarded by a dragon whose coils encircle her castle; and only the man who slays the dragon can win her for his bride. But Ragnar Lodbrog, who so wins her, is still the son of Sigurdr. Thora dies; and Ragnar at length woos the beautiful Kraka, whom, however, he is on the point of deserting for the daughter of Östen, when Kraka reveals herself as the child of Sigurdr and Brenhyldr. The myth has been weakened in its extension; but the half-consciousness of its origin is betrayed in the very names and the incidents of the story, even as in the Iliad the tears which

Sigurdr can be wounded only in one spot, as the bright sun of summer cannot grow dim till it is pierced by the thorn of winter. Like Phœbus who smites the dragon at Pytho, the Northern hero slays the serpent Fafnir, and wins back the treasure of the Niflungar, while he rouses Brenhyldr from her long slumber. This treasure is the power of vegetation which has been lulled to sleep by the mists and clouds of winter, the seeds which refuse to grow while Dêmêtêr sorrows for her child Persephonê. The desertion of Brenhyldr is the advance of spring into summer; and from it follows of necessity the hatred of Brenhyldr for Gudrun who has stolen away the love of Sigurdr.[1] A dark doom presses heavily on him, darker and more woful than that which weighed down the

---

Eôs sheds on the death of Memnon are 'morning dew.' See Mr. Thorpe's valuable work on Northern Mythology, vol. i. pp. 108, 113. Mr. Thorpe is aware of the resemblance of the Northern mythology to that of the Greeks, but he seems scarcely to have understood its extent. In his explanations he inclines (vol. i. p. 122, &c.) to the opinion that real historical events have given rise to myths, a conclusion which Mr. Grote refuses to admit. But his method throws no light on the cause of these resemblances between the mythological systems of nations utterly severed from one another; still less does it show why they should in each case assume their particular form, and why it is that they could have assumed no other.

[1] It is but another form of the jealousy of Eôs and Procris. It finds its most tender expression in the grief of Œnônê for the faithlessness of Paris.

toiling Heracles; for the labour of Heracles issued always in victory, but Sigurdr must win his own wife Brenhyldr only to hand her over to Gunnar. The sun must deliver the bright Spring, whom he had wooed and won, to the gloomy powers of cold and darkness. Gudrun only remains; but though outwardly she is fair and bright, she is of kin to the wintry beings; for the late summer is more closely allied to death than to life. Yet Gunnar, her brother, cannot rest; the wrath of the cold has been roused, and he resolves to slay the bright and beautiful Sigurdr. The deed is done by Gunnar's brethren, the cloud, the wind, and the storm; and Brenhyldr, filled again with her early love, lies down to die with him who had forsaken her.[1]

[1] Mr. Dasent, who has very ably traced out the intimate connection of the mythological systems of the Aryan race, seems, like Mr. Gladstone, to attribute their repulsive aspects to a moral cause. His reasons, however, are very different. The incessant display of the Hellenic and Teutonic gods he attributes to a consciousness on the part of their worshippers that they were *subjective*, and hence unsubstantial. He contrasts rightly the 'restlessness' of a false religion 'when brought face to face with the quiet dignity and majesty of the' true; but his instances appear to be scarcely in point. The manifestations of Moloch, Chemosh, and Milcom, may originate in such a feeling; but we cannot at once assign a moral and a mythological origin to those of Zeus and Odin, Thor and Vishnu. If Zeus and Odin were once the heaven, or the sky, then their human personification must, as we have seen, be followed by the development of

F

In the brighter land which was the home of the Hellenic race on either side of the Ægæan Sea, the national songs would be founded on mythical phrases telling not of the yearly birth and death of Nature, but of the daily course of the sun. With this one dif-

<small>Groundwork of the Iliad.</small>

their special mythical attributes and history, and could have been followed by no others. The idea of the mighty sun toiling for weak and worthless men would inevitably be developed into the strong Herakles, brave or coarse, grave or even comic, virtuous or immoral. The adventures of Zeus may be 'tinged with all the lust and guile which the wickedness of the natural man planted on a hotbed of iniquity is capable of conceiving;' but we shall scarcely trace them to a religious perversion, if we accept the conclusions which a comparison of Greek mythology with the earliest Vedic literature forces upon us. The main difference between the adventures of Odin and Zeus is that, while those of the latter are chiefly erotic, the former involve the exhibition of gigantic physical strength, — a distinction at once accounted for by differences of soil and climate. See Dasent, Popular Tales from the Norse, Introduction, p. lix.

Whether the Beast epic of the North had its origin in a Nature-worship, is a question which it may perhaps be difficult to determine; but, as with the mythical history of the gods, Mr. Dasent appears to include in the various Beast epics of the Aryan races some instances which seem not to belong to it. Thus, as illustrating the transformation of men into beasts, he alleges Europa and her bull, Leda and her swan. (Popular Tales from the Norse, Introduction, p. xix). If it be an illustration, it accounts for all such transformations; but it does so in a way which is completely subversive of any hypothesis of Nature-worship. The bull of Europa is the sun, bearing the light to the Western land. In the Vedas the image of a bull is ference, the story of the Volsunga Saga and the Nibelungen Lied lies at the root of the epic to which the poet of the Greek heroic ages has imparted such wonderful consistency and beauty.[1]

very commonly employed as expressing the power and speed of the sun. In the same way, the sun was spoken of as a horse, and the head of the horse appears in the legend of Kephalos and Procris. Again, the horses of the sun were called Harits; and in these we have the prototype of the Greek charites,— an inverse transmutation, for while in the other instances the human is changed into a brute personality, in this the beasts are converted into maidens. The same process seems to have been at work in producing the Greek god of love, Erôs. Max Müller, Comparative Mythology, pp. 53, 81, &c.

The mythical character of the herds of the sun (the bright morning clouds) subverts Mr. Gladstone's supposition that the cattle of Helios are likewise a relic of Nature-worship. Homer and the Homeric Age, vol. ii. p. 412. Tales from Greek Mythology, p. 118.

[1] It is impossible to read Dr. Thirlwall's remarks (History of Greece, vol. i. ch. v.) on the Trojan legend without noting the sound judgment which sees at once the ground on which the battle of Homeric credibility must be fought out. Mr. Grote has shown that, if the tale of Troy rests on any historical basis, the evidence which may establish this is wholly beyond our reach, and that, if truth may be mixed up with fable, the attempt to extricate it is visionary. But it is quite as difficult to deny Dr. Thirlwall's assertion that 'even if unfounded, it must still have had some adequate occasion and motive.' In the absence of a better explanation, there was no alternative but to connect it with quarrels arising out of the Greek colonies in Asia. But this hypothesis only renders more mysterious and perplexing the resemblance, or rather the identity, of this legend with that of the Volsunga Saga and the Nibelungen Lied. If we do not

Yet we cannot but see that the tale as handled by him does not exhibit its earliest form, and that he has adopted as much of the popular mythology as suited his purpose, and no more. If casual expressions throughout the poem leave no room to doubt that he knew of wars among the heavenly beings, of the dethronement of Kronos, of the good service and the hard recompense of Prometheus, and the early death of Achilles, it appears not less manifest that the idea of Œnone and of her relations with Paris could not have dawned for the first time on the mind of a later age. It was no part of the poet's design to exhibit a complete mythology; and the Iliad exhibits only that process of disintegration which was perpetually multiplying new tales and new beings from the old mythical language. Achilles, Meleagros, Memnon, Bellerophon, and Sarpedon, are all creations from the same fruitful stock; but Achilles himself, with all his greatness and all his glory, is the centre only of that part of the myth which recounts his exploits in the Iliad. In the original legend the real groundwork of the tale was the life and death of Paris, the bright and changeful sun. It is impossible not to see the

look now for any solution of political history, Comparative Mythology has furnished another from the history of the human mind, which would probably commend itself to Dr. Thirlwall as at once more adequate and convincing.

common characteristics which amidst all their divergences are manifested in Paris, Achilles, and Meleagros. If Paris in the Iliad is exhibited as mean and effeminate, his very name Alexandros is at once the evidence that he had not been so from the first. Otherwise, in all the three we have the same strange and capricious alternations of moody sullenness and brilliant action,— the veiling of the sun under the dark and lowering storm-cloud. There was a time when the tale began with the strange signs and dreams which went before the birth of Paris. From the dark night was to spring the fiery and flaming sun; and the dream of Hecabê [1] brought before her the torch as the emblem of her unborn child. It is needless to interpret every detail in the countless forms which such myths assume. The sorrows with which the life of Paris began may or may not have been suggested by the battle of the sun with the dark clouds which often gather round him at his rising; but if such be the struggle, it ended in victory, and the early career of Paris is one of unbroken glory and beneficence. His path is gilded with the tender light

[1] The character of Hecabé is as completely negative among the Trojans as is that of Lêto among the immortal inhabitants of Olympus. The reason is for both the same. Both are but embodiments of the silent and colourless night from which is to spring the glowing sun.

of love; he looks down on the bright child of the happy waters, and she returns his greeting with a glad and ready smile. His countenance is still gentle and loving, while his arm is strong and his heart brave. Wherever he goes, he awakens a deep gratitude and joy, and men call him Alexandros because he scares away the unknown perils of secresy and darkness. But the charms of early morning lose their power; lands yet unseen tempt him to wander far away and to leave the bright Œnone. She was fair, but further towards the West was the abode of one, if not fairer, yet brighter and more glorious. The words of Aphroditê have done their work. The morning which gladdened him with a virgin love is cast aside for the gaudy and flaunting day; and Œnone must give way to Helen. It is but another form of the tale of Kephalos, Procris, and Eôs; while the vengeance taken by the kinsfolk of Helen is but the punishment which Sigurdr brings upon himself when he has forsaken Brenhyldr for the child of Gunnar.[1] On this foundation might be raised the legend of a long and fearful strife; and what magnificent proportions such a legend might assume, is attested by the poem which sings of the struggle and victory of

---

[1] Thus Agamemnon and Menelaos, with their allies, would stand in the place of the more forbidding Gunnar, Hogni, and Hodr, &c., of the Northern epic.

Achilles and Agamemnon in the land of the rising sun. It matters not that Achilles himself is but a reflection of the enemy against whom he fights. There was nothing in such an incident to violate the law of mythological credibility; and apart from this, the inventive faculty was not restrained from interweaving independent mythical details into one consecutive story. But by the transfer of his love to Helen a change comes over the spirit of Paris; the unclouded sun has passed behind the veil. The bright hero, who in his early years had been the defender of his countrymen, now lies at ease on silken couches, while others suffer for his sin. The glory is hidden, yet not wholly lost, for Paris sits in his secret chamber, burnishing his golden armour, making ready for the fight, yet doing nothing. But the victory of Agamemnon is not less sure than that of Gunnar. The sun long clouded must sink in darkness and disaster; and Paris is smitten with arrows taken from his own quiver, which Heracles has bequeathed to the Achæan hero. But with the fatal wound comes back his love for the lost Œnonê; and, not less forgiving than Procris to the faithless Kephalos, Œnone stands before him. With a soft and tender grief she gazes on the face which once had filled the whole earth for her with beauty. She sees his lifeblood flowing away; but though she is of the bright race of the

gods, and though she has the power of the soft
evening time to soothe the woes of mortal men,
she cannot heal the poisoned wound which is
slaying Paris, as the deadly thorn and mistletoe
slew the bright Gunnar and Baldr the fair and
pure. But with the death of him who once was
called Alexandros, the light of her life is gone.
Paris rests in the sleep of death, and Œnone
lies lifeless by his side (XXVI.).[1]

It is the Volsung tale, as wrought out by the
poets of a bright and fertile land.[2] Yet, if the

---

[1] The authorship of the Iliad is a vexed question into which there is no need to enter here at any length. If it is absurd to assume a multitude of authors, the internal evidence of the poem, even after all the counter arguments of Colonel Mure and Mr. Gladstone, seems unquestionably to uphold Mr. Grote's conclusion that at the least we have in it an Iliad and an Achilleis combined. As Mr. Grote admits, it is quite possible that both these poems may have one author; but if their groundwork be the same as that of the Volsung tale and the Nibelungen Lied, it appears rather to raise a presumption against it. With all our efforts, we cannot throw ourselves back into the mental state of the heroic ages; and it is very unsafe for us to infer that there cannot have been many contemporary bards who might have been authors even of the Iliad. Many of the episodes are undoubtedly distinct legends, which may or may not have been composed by the author of the rest of the poem.

[2] The mythology of Greece can no longer be regarded as the exponent of abstruse physical truths or theories. There can be no doubt that (whatever appearance of such a system may have been imparted to it by the priests) the supposition does not apply with more force even to Egyptian mythology. There, as well as in Greece and Northern Europe, we have again the solar

harsh climate of the North modified the Norse
mythology, it also moulded indefinitely
the national character, and the two acted
and reacted on each other. Bred up to
fight with Nature in a constant battle for

<small>Comparison of Greek and Norse mythology.</small>

<hr>

legend. The spring was the time of festival, the autumn of fast
and mourning. It would almost seem as though the Egyptian
myths were in this respect more closely akin to those of Northern
than of Southern Europe. See Milman, History of Christianity,
vol. i. p. 13. Compare also the Surtr of the Icelandic Mythology, Dasent's Norsemen in Iceland, Oxford Essays for 1858,
p. 198.

The groundwork of the Volsunga Saga, of the tales of Paris,
Helen, and Œnônê, reappears in the legends and the worship of
Adonis. The origin of the myth is in this case self-evident,
while the grossness of the forms which it has assumed shows the
degree to which such legends may either influence or be modified by national characteristics or the physical conditions of
a country. Even in their worst aspects, Zeus and Odin retain
some majesty and manly power; but in the legend of Adonis,
the idea of the sun as calling the earth back to life has been
sensualised to a degree far beyond the sensuousness of Greek or
Teutonic mythology. In fact, the image of Dêmêtêr has passed
by a very easy transmutation into that of Aphroditê; but there
remains not only the early death of Adonis, but it is assigned to
the very cause which cuts short the life of Achilles, Sigurdr,
Baldr, Paris, and Meleagros. The boar's tusk is but the thorn
of winter and the poisoned robe of Herakles; and accordingly
there were versions which affirmed that it was Apollo who in
the form of a boar killed the darling of Aphroditê. The division
of time also varies. In some legends the covenant is the same
as that which is made with Dêmêtêr for Persephonê. In others,
he remains four months in Hades, four with Aphroditê, and the
remaining four, being at his own disposal, he chooses to spend

existence, the Norseman became fearless, honest, and truthful, ready to smite and ready to forgive, shrinking not from pain himself, and careless of inflicting it on others. Witnessing everywhere the struggle of conflicting forces, he was tempted to look on life as a field for warfare, and to own no law for those who were not bound with him in ties of blood and friendship. Hence there was impressed on him a stern and fierce character, exaggerated not unfrequently into a gross and brutal cruelty; and his national songs reflected the repulsive not less than the fairer aspect of his disposition. In the Volsung tale, as in the later epics, there is much of feud, jealousy, and bloodshed, much which to the mind of a less tumultuous age must be simply distasteful or even horrible. To what extent this may be owing to their own character, it may perhaps be difficult to determine; yet it would seem rash to lay to their charge the special kinds of evil dealing of which we read in their great national legends. Mr. Dasent, who accounts for the immoral or repulsive details of Greek mythology entirely on

with the latter. But the myth had been not merely corrupted; it was poisoned by the touch of Oriental sensuality. In the Volsung tale, Sigurdr dies as pure, as lives the Hellenic Phœbus: in the Eastern myth, from Adonis springs Priapus. The mourning of the women for Tammuz might well rouse the righteous indignation of the Hebrew prophet. The hymn of Dêmêtêr would have called forth from him a rebuke less severe.

moral and religious grounds, has consistently assigned a purpose not less didactic to the mythology of the North. In the Volsung tale he sees simply men and women, whose history had never grown out of conditions not belonging to human life. It speaks to him of love and hate, of 'all that can foster passion or beget revenge. Ill-assorted marriages, . . . envyings, jealousies, hatreds, murders, all the works of the natural man, combine together to form that marvellous story which begins with a curse, the curse of ill-gotten gold; and ends with a curse, a widow's curse, which drags down all on whom it falls, and even her own flesh and blood, to a certain doom.'[1] This picture, of which the composition has been so strangely and fully laid bare by the results of comparative mythology, is perhaps no fair representation of the Norseman. It is not easy to believe that the relations between Sigurdr and Gunnar were (even rarely) realised in the actual life of the Norwegian or the Icelander. But, in his eagerness to defend their domestic morality, Mr. Dasent appears to be hurried into something like injustice to the society of the Greek heroic ages. These ages, to him, are polished and false[2], a period in which woman was

[1] Popular Tales from the Norse, Introduction, p. lxi.
[2] Ibid. p. lxxiv.

a toy, whereas she was a helpmeet to the Teuton, a time in which men lacked in general the feelings of natural affection. If the words refer to a later age, the comparison is scarcely relevant; and of the Homeric society the picture is scarcely true. The feelings of friendship are even exaggerated in Achilles; the pure freedom of domestic equality is brought out with winning lustre in Nausicaâ and Penelopê. But whether with the Greek or the Norseman, all judgment is premature until we have decided whether we are or are not dealing with legends which, whether in whole or in part, have sprung from the mythical expressions of a forgotten language. We can draw no inference from the actions of Zeus or Heracles as to the character of the Greeks; we cannot take the fatal quarrels of Brenhyldr, Gunnar, and Sigurdr, as any evidence of the character of the Norseman.

Living in a land of ice-bound fjords and desolate fells, hearing the mournful wail of the waving pine branches, looking on the stern strife of frost and fire, witnessing year by year the death of the short-lived summer, the Norseman was inured to sombre if not gloomy thought, to the rugged independence of the country as opposed to the artificial society of a town. His own sternness was but

Special characteristics of Greek mythology.

the reflection of the land in which he lived; and
it was reflected, in its turn, in the tales which he
told whether of the heroes or the gods. The
Greek, dwelling in sunnier regions, where the
interchange of summer and winter brought with
it no feelings of overpowering gloom, exhibited
in his words and songs the happiness which he
experienced in himself. Caring less, perhaps, to
hold communion with the silent mountains and
the heaving sea, he was drawn to the life of
cities, where he could share his joys and sorrows
with his kinsmen. The earth was his mother;
the gods who dwelt on Olympus had the likeness
of men without their pains or their doom of death.
There Zeus sat on his golden throne, and beside
him was the glorious Apollo, not the deified man[1],
but the sun-god invested with a human personality. But (with whatever modifications caused
by climate and circumstances) both were inheri-
tors of a common mythology, which with much
that was beautiful and good united also much

[1] The common mythology of the whole Aryan race goes
against the supposition that Apollo and Athênê owe their existence to man-worship and woman-worship respectively: but
Athênê is an embodiment simply of moral and intellectual greatness. The absence or deterioration of the former converts Athênê
into the Colchian Medeia. The latter type, when still further
degraded, becomes the Latin Canidia, a close approximation to
the common witch of more modern superstition.

that was repulsive and immoral.[1] Both, from the ordinary speech of their common forefathers, had framed a number of legends which had their gross and impure aspects, but for the grossness of which they were not (as we have seen), and they could not be, responsible.

But if the mythology of the Greeks is in sub-

[1] In his analysis of the Volsung tale, Mr. Dasent very ably traces the marks left by the national character on the Norse mythology; but he scarcely brings into sufficient prominence that after all it was only modification, not invention. Sigurdr is the very reverse of the orientalised Adonis; but the intermediate link is supplied by the Hellenic Phœbus. In describing Sigurdr, Mr. Dasent, perhaps unconsciously, falls into the Homeric phrases which speak of the glorious sun-god. His beautiful limbs, his golden hair, the piercing eye of which few dared to meet the gaze, are all characteristics of the Homeric Apollo; to these are undoubtedly added the hardier virtues of the North, which may to us make the picture more attractive, and which appear in some degree to soften in Mr. Dasent's eyes the harshness and extreme intricacy of the Northern mythology. The sequence of motives and incidents is such as might perplex or even utterly baffle the reader. It is impossible to know what is coming; the ordinary conditions of society wholly fail to explain the actions and purposes of the chief actors in the story, and we are left at a loss to know how such a tangled web of inscrutable adventures could ever have been woven by the fancy of man. The key to the mythology of Greece also unlocks that of the North. The mystery is substantially explained; but with the discovery comes the conclusion that the groundwork of the story is not peculiar to the Norse, and that its special forms of cause and effect do not therefore represent the ordinary motives and conditions of their social life.

stance and in development the same as that of the North, they differed widely in their later history. That of the Greeks passed through the stages of growth, maturity, and decay, without any violent external repression.[1] The mythical language of the earliest age had supplied them with an inexhaustible fountain of legendary narrative; and the tales so framed had received an implicit belief, which, though intense and unquestioning, could scarcely be called religious, and in no sense could be regarded as moral. And just because the belief accorded to it was not moral, the time came gradually when thoughtful men rose (through earnest effort, rather we would say, through Divine guidance) to the conviction of higher and clearer truth. If even the Greek of the heroic age found in his mythology neither a rule of life nor the ideal of that Deity whom in his heart he really worshipped, still less would this be the case with the poets and philosophers of later times. To Æschylus Zeus was but the mere name[2] of a God whose actions were not those of the son of Kronos; to Sophocles it made no difference whether He were called Zeus or by any other name, as long as he might retain the con-

Full development of Greek mythology.

[1] The subject is fully examined by Mr. Grote, History of Greece, vol. i. ch. xvii.
[2] Agamemnon, 160.

viction of His eternity and His righteousness.[1] If from his own moral perception Pindar refused to credit charges of gluttony against the gods, no violent shock was given to the popular belief; and even Socrates might teach the strictest responsibility of man to a perfectly impartial Judge, even while he spoke of the mythical tribunal of Minos, Rhadamanthus, and Æacos.[2] He was accused, indeed, of introducing new gods: this charge he denied, and perhaps truly; but in no sense whatever was he a worshipper of the Olympian Zeus, or of the Phœbus who smote the Pythian dragon.

As compared with the Greek, the mythology of Northern Europe was arrested almost in its middle growth. After a fierce struggle, Christianity was forced upon the reluctant Northmen, long before poets had risen among them to whom the sensuality or ferocity of their mythology was repulsive or revolting, long before philosophers had evolved a body of moral belief, by the side of which the popular mythology might continue peacefully to exist. By a sudden revolution, Odin and the Æsir, the deities of the North, were hurled from their ancient thrones, before the dread twilight

Arrested growth of Northern mythology.

---

[1] Sophocles, Œd. Tyr. 903.
[2] See the Gorgias of Plato, lxxx.

of the gods[1] had come. Henceforth they could only be regarded either as men or devils. The former alternative made Odin a descendant of Noah[2]; by the latter the celestial hierarchy became malignant spirits riding on the storm-cloud and the whirlwind. If these gods had sometimes been beneficent before, they were never beneficent now. All that was beautiful and good in the older belief had been transferred to the Christian ideals of chivalry and saintliness, which furnished a boundless field and inexhaustible nourishment for the most exuberant inventive faculty.[3] The demons of Hesiod were the spirits of the good who had died the painless death of the Golden Age; but even in heathen times they were gradually invested with a malignant character.[4] With Thor and Odin the transmutation was more rapid and complete; and Frigga and Freya became beings full of a wisdom and power

---

[1] This idea Mr. Dasent seems to regard too exclusively as a characteristic of Teutonic mythology. (Popular Tales of the Norse, Introduction, pp. lvii., lxxv.) It is undoubtedly embodied in the Æschylean legend of Prometheus, although other versions accounted for his deliverance without the deposition of Zeus.

[2] Grote, History of Greece, vol. i. p. 624.

[3] Ibid. p. 628. M. de Montalembert's History, "Les Moines d'Occident," is a storehouse of legends belonging to the ideal of saintliness. He appears, however, to treat some of them rather in the spirit of Euêmerus. See Edinburgh Review, No. cxxxii. Oct. 1861, p. 339.

[4] Grote, History of Greece, vol. i. p. 96.

which they used only for evil. The same character passed to those who were or professed to be their votaries; and the assumption of an unlawful knowledge paved the way for that persecution of a fictitious witchcraft which has stamped an indelible disgrace on mediæval Christendom.[1]

So marvellous is that chronicle of heathen mythology, as it lies spread out before us in the light of the ancient speech,—marvellous not only as showing how nations, utterly severed from each other, preserved their common inheritance, but as laying bare that early condition of thought without which mythology could never have had a being. Yet, if it has much to astonish us, it has nothing to bewilder or even to perplex, for the simultaneous development of the same myths by countless tribes unknown to each other would be a marvel too vast even for the greediest credulity to swallow,—a standing miracle without purpose and

Light thrown on both by the Vedic poems.

---

[1] See Mr. Dasent's very able sketch of the origin and development of the modern ideas of witchcraft. (Popular Tales from the Norse, Introduction, p. cvii. &c. &c.)

It was this idea of a knowledge gained unlawfully from evil spirits, which, far more perhaps than a habit of submission to Church authority, impeded or repressed all researches in physical science. Gerbert of Ravenna (Sylvester II.) and Roger Bacon alike acquired a reputation of dabbling in diabolical lore. In the time of Galileo, the accusers confined themselves to the simple charge of an unlawful use of human intellect.

without meaning.[1] To the earliest records of Aryan literature is due the wonderful discovery that the vehement accusations of Christian controversialists and the timid explanations of heathen apologists were alike unfounded [2], that the impersonations of the old mythology had no substantial existence, and that the mythical narratives which grew up around them were not wrought out by a vile and corrupt imagination deliberately profaning the deposit of a revealed truth which it was hopeless that they should understand. To the language of the early Vedic

---

[1] Professor Max Müller rightly remarks that 'the idea of a humanity emerging slowly from the depths of an animal brutality can never be maintained again.' (Comparative Mythology, p. 5.) But if the history of language puts an end to such a theory, it does not so immediately determine whether mythology was developed consciously or unconsciously. Professor Müller has shown forcibly that the deliberate invention of absurd stories about the gods implies a period of temporary insanity, coming over all nations at the same time, which is an utter anomaly in the history of the human mind. It is indeed difficult to suppose that the people 'who produced men like Thales, Heracleitos, and Pythagoras, should have consisted of idle talkers but a few centuries before the time of these sages.' But it is far more difficult to imagine that the high moral standard of the latter could have been preceded by so gross and loathsome a degradation of mind and spirit, which such an hypothesis would assume. The supposition seems to be not merely difficult but impossible.

[2] See Grote, History of Greece, vol. i. p. 15, &c.

poems we owe our knowledge that the development of such a mythology was inevitable, and that the phrases of that early speech, when their original meaning was once forgotten or misapprehended, would give rise to just those coarse, sensual, and immoral images, from which the purer feeling of later times would instinctively recoil.

Step by step this analysis of mythology leads us back to what would seem to be the earliest condition of the human mind, and from that onwards through the mythopœic age to the philosophy of historical Greece. On the general character of its course there can be no doubt, nor is the question materially affected by the hypothesis that a period of pure monotheism intervened between the earliest time and that which multiplied the mythical inhabitants of Asgard or Olympus.[1] In one sense the supposition may be true: in another it might be truer to say that the monotheism so attained never died away. It was impossible that any real fetiche worship could arise while man had not arranged his first conceptions with regard to the nature of all material things or even to his own. If from the consciousness of his own existence he attributed the same existence to all outward objects, he did so, as we have

Stages in the growth of mythical systems.

[1] Dasent, Popular Tales from the Norse, Introduction, p. lxvii.

seen, without drawing any distinctions between consciousness and personality. The idea of their divinity in any sense would be an inference, not a sensation; and the analysis of language, which shows that all predicative words are the expression of general ideas [1], does not show us that the human mind was immediately exercised by any train of connected reasoning. If, however, this earliest state was not followed by one which invested outward things with a personal life, if in some way men could believe in a malignant yet unconscious and unsentient power residing in stones and rocks, there would at once be developed a fetiche worship, the most degrading and the most hopeless, which, if expanded at all, could issue out only in a polytheism of devils. Yet even here some faint perceptions might remain of moral qualities,—unless we believe that the Divine likeness may be wholly blotted out; but is it possible to account for the loathsome earthliness of some forms of heathenism, except by the hypothesis that on them the idea of Deity has never dawned? But if, when gradually awakened, the consciousness of their own personality might lead others to attribute the same personal life to outward objects, the deification of these objects or powers would not follow as an immediate or even as a necessary conse-

[1] Max Müller, On the Science of Language, Lect. IX.

quence. For a long time they might scarcely be conscious of the degree to which they personified them; or they might continue to look upon them as beings condemned to the same life of toil and trouble with themselves. Such a thought, it is obvious, might lead at once to the idea of One (distinct from all that they saw or heard) who ordained this life of labour; and the conviction of a supreme God, the Maker of all things visible and sensible, might take possession of the mind[1]; but it is not less clear that such a conviction would not necessarily affect their ideas as to what they saw in the world around them. The Sun in all his various aspects, the Morning, the Evening, and the Night, might become more and more personal, even while the belief in a God exalted high above all might continue to gain strength. In other words, the foundation of their moral belief would at once be distinct from the foundation of their future mythology. Still, except to the thoughtful few, the personality of the great objects of the natural world would be more and more exalted, even while it assumed more and more a strictly human form. The result would be a polytheism of anthropomor-

---

[1] This state might also easily pass into Eastern dualism. The development of the Hellenic mind was more wholesome. The prevalence of evil never led it to regard evil as co-ordinate with good.

phous gods, in which the chief divinities would be the heaven and the sun.[1] To the former, as covering and shielding all things, would be assigned those attributes which almost make us look on the Olympian Zeus and the Teutonic Alfadir[2] as faint reflections of Him who has made and loves mankind. But for neither the majesty of Zeus or Odin, nor for the unsullied purity of Phœbus Apollo, of Athênê or of Artemis, need we look further than to mythical phrases which spoke once of Dyaus, Varuna, and Indra.

So might a mythology the most intricate, and a moral belief entirely independent of it, go on side by side. For the former had not sprung up from any religious conviction; and the latter might advance beyond the stage of infancy, before the corruption of the true mythical speech led to the multiplication of mythological narratives. In the absence of any historical sense or any written literature, these tales would be eagerly welcomed, and disseminated without a doubt of their truth. But the national

Mythology not strictly a religious belief.

---

[1] It is easy also to see how a substantial conviction of the Divine Unity might co-exist with the worship of his manifestation under the image of fire, the Vedic *Agni* (Ignis). This is again a belief founded on the sun as the all-seeing eye of day.

[2] Dasent, Norsemen in Iceland, in Oxford Essays for 1858, p. 187.

character might exhibit many good and noble qualities, even while that of its greatest mythical heroes stood indefinitely lower. The moody sullenness, the implacable passion, and the ferocious cruelty of Achilles, the capricious jealousy, idleness, and activity of Meleagros, are wellnigh incredible; nor is there any evidence either that these qualities were common amongst the Greeks in the heroic age, or that they attracted any great admiration or esteem. It can be no subject of regret to learn that they were as little responsible for the moral standard of Achilles and Meleagros as for that of Zeus and Heracles; and that the idea of each originated as little with them as the conception of Odin and Baldr, of Sigurdr and Gunnar, originated in the mind of the Teuton. So might the Spirit of God work in the human heart, even while a vast fabric of mythology was assuming proportions more and more colossal and systematic; so, in spite of sensual gods, the thought of whom made the poet shudder, might the real faith both of the poet and his hearers in an unseen Father continue substantially unshaken. So, while he cared not to avow any disbelief in mythical stories of Niobê or Prometheus, Socrates might tell of One who made men and watched over them for their good, and by the aid of that unseen God strive to keep his hands clean and his heart pure.

TALES OF THE GODS AND HEROES

KEPHALOS AND PROCRIS.[1]

OF all the maidens in the land of Attica none was so beautiful as Procris, the daughter of King Erectheus. She was the delight of her father's heart, not so much for her beauty as for her goodness and her gentleness. The sight of her fair face, and the sound of her happy voice, brought gladness to all who saw and heard her. Every one stopped to listen to the songs which she sang as she sat working busily at the loom; and the maidens who dwelt with her were glad when the hour came to go with Procris and wash their clothes[2] or draw water from the fountain.[3] Then, when all her tasks were ended, she would roam over hill and valley, into every nook and dell. There was no spot in all the land where Procris had not been. She lay down to rest on the top of the highest hills, or by the side of the stream where it murmured among the rocks far down in the woody glen. So passed her days away; and while all loved her and rejoiced to see her face, only Procris knew not of her own beauty, and thought not of her own goodness. But they amongst whom she lived, the old and the young, the sorrowful and the happy, all said that Procris, the child of Hersê [1], was always as fair and bright as the dew of early morning.

Once in her many wanderings she had climbed the heights of Mount Hymettos, almost before the first streak of dawn was seen in the sky. Far away, as she looked over the blue sea, her eyes rested on the glittering cliffs and white shore of Eubœa, and as she looked she saw that a ship was sailing towards the shore beneath the hill of Hymettos. Presently it reached the shore, and she could see that a man stepped out of the ship, and began to climb the hill, while the rest remained on the beach. As he came nearer to her, Procris knew that his face was very fair, and she thought that she had never seen such beauty in mortal man before. She had heard that sometimes the gods come down from their home on Olympus to mingle among the children of men, and that sometimes the bright heroes were seen in the places where they had lived on the earth before they were taken to dwell in the halls of Zeus. As the stranger came near to her, the sun rose up brightly and without a cloud from the dark sea; and its light fell on his face, and made

it gleam with more than mortal beauty. Gently
he came towards her, and said, 'O lady, I am
come from the far-off eastern land; and as I drew
near to this shore, I saw that some one was resting
here upon the hill. So I hastened to leave the ship,
that I might learn the name of the country which
I have reached. My name is Kephalos, and my
father Hêlios lives in a beautiful home beyond
the sea; but I am travelling over the earth, till
I shall have gone over every land and seen all
the cities which men have built. Tell me now
thy name, and the name of this fair land.' Then
she said, 'O stranger, my name is Procris, and I
am the daughter of King Erectheus, who dwells at
Athens yonder, where thou seest the bright line
of Kephisos flowing gently towards the sea.' So
Procris guided the stranger to her father's house;
and Erectheus received him kindly, and spread
a banquet before him. But as they feasted and
drank the dark red wine, he thought almost that
Kephalos must be one of the bright heroes come
back to his own land, so fair and beautiful was
he to look upon, and that none save only his
own child Procris might be compared to him for
beauty.

Long time Kephalos abode in the house of
Erectheus, and, each day, he loved more and

more the bright and happy Procris; and Procris became brighter and happier, as the eye of Kephalos rested gently and lovingly upon her. At last Kephalos told her of his love, and Erectheus gave him his child to be his wife; and there were none in all the land who dwelt together in a love so deep and pure as that of Kephalos and Procris.

But among the maidens of that land there was one who was named Eôs.[5] She too was fair and beautiful; but she had not the gentle spirit and the guileless heart of Procris. Whenever Kephalos wandered forth with his young wife, then Eôs would seek to follow them stealthily; or, if she met them by chance, she would suffer her eyes to rest long on the fair face of Kephalos, till she began to envy the happiness of Procris. And so one day, when there was a feast of the people of the land and the maidens danced on the soft grass around the fountain, Kephalos and Eôs talked together; and Eôs suffered herself to be carried away by her evil love. From that day she sought more and more to talk with Kephalos, till at last she bowed her head before him and told him softly of her love. But Kephalos said to her gently, 'O maiden, thou art fair to look upon, and there are others who may love thee well, and thou deservest the love of any. But I may not leave Procris, whom Erectheus has given to me to be my wife. Forgive me, maiden, if Procris appear to me even fairer than thou art; but I prize her gentleness more than her beauty, and Procris with her pure love and guileless heart shall be always dearer to me than any other in all the wide earth.' Then Eôs answered him craftily, 'O Kephalos, thou hast suffered thyself to be deceived. Procris loves thee not as I do; prove her love, and thou shalt see that I have spoken truly.'

Thus Eôs spake to him for many days; and the great happiness of his life was marred, for the words of Eôs would come back to his mind, as he looked on the happy and guileless Procris. He had begun to doubt whether she were in very deed so pure and good as she seemed to be; and at last he said to Eôs that he would prove her love. Then Eôs told him how to do so, and said that if he came before his wife as a stranger, and brought to her rich gifts as from a distant land, she would forget her love for Kephalos.

With a heavy heart he went away, for he foreboded evil days from the subtle words of Eôs; and he departed and dwelt in another land. So the time passed on, until many weeks and months had gone by, and Procris mourned and wept in the house of Erectheus, until the brightness of her eye was dimmed and her voice had lost its gladness. Day after day she sought throughout all the land for Kephalos; day after day she went up the hill of Hymettos, and as she looked towards the sea, she said, 'Surely he will come back again; ah, Kephalos, thou knowest not the love which thou hast forsaken.' Thus she pined away in her sorrow, although to all who were around her she was as gentle and as loving as ever. Her father was now old and weak, and he knew that he must soon die; but it grieved him most of all that he must leave his child in a grief more bitter than if Kephalos had remained to comfort her. So Erectheus died, and the people honoured him as one of the heroes of the land; but Procris remained in his house desolate, and all who saw her pitied her for her true love and her deep sorrow. At last she felt that Kephalos would return no more, and that she would no more be happy until she went to her father in the bright home of the heroes and the gods.

Then a look of peace and loving patience came over her fair face; and she roamed with a strange gladness through every place where Kephalos had wandered with her; and so it came to pass that one day Procris sat resting in the early morning on the eastern slopes of Mount Hymettos, when suddenly she beheld a man coming near to her. The dress was strange, but she half thought that she knew his tall form and the light step as he came up the hill. Presently he came close to her, and she felt as if she were in a strange dream. The sight of his face and the glance of his eye carried her back to the days that were past, and she started up and ran towards him, saying, 'O Kephalos, thou art come back at last; how couldst thou forsake me so long?' But the stranger answered, in a low and gentle voice (for he saw that she was in great sorrow), 'O lady, thou art deceived. I am a stranger come from a far country, and I seek to know the name of this land.' Then Procris sat down again on the grass, and clasped her hands and said slowly, 'It is changed, and I cannot tell how; yet surely it is the voice of Kephalos.' Then she turned to the stranger and said, 'O stranger, I am mourning for Kephalos whom I have loved and lost; he too came from a far land across the eastern sea. Dost thou know him, and canst thou tell me where I may find him?' And the stranger answered, 'I know him, lady; he is again in his own home far away, whither thou canst not go; yet think not of him, for he has forgotten his love.' Then the stranger spoke to her in gentle and soothing words, until her grief became less bitter. Long time he abode in the land; and it pleased Procris to hear his voice while his eye rested kindly on her, until she almost fancied that she was with Kephalos once more. And she thought within herself, 'What must that land be, from which there can come two who are as beautiful as the bright heroes?'

So at last, when with soft and gentle words he had soothed her sorrow, the stranger spoke to her of his love; and Procris felt that she too could love him, for had not Kephalos despised her love and forsaken her long ago? So he said, 'Canst thou love me, Procris, instead of Kephalos?' and when she gently answered 'Yes,' then a change came over the face of the stranger, and she saw that it was Kephalos himself who clasped her in his arms. With a wild cry she broke from him, and as bitter tears ran down her cheek, she said, 'O Kephalos, Kephalos, why hast thou done thus? All my love was thine; and *thou* hast drawn me into evil deeds.' Then, without tarrying for his answer, with all her strength she fled away; and she hastened to the sea-shore, and bade them make ready a ship to take her from her father's land. Sorrowfully they did as she besought them, and they took her to the island of Crete far away in the eastern sea.

When Procris was gone, the maiden Eôs came and stood before Kephalos, and she said to him, 'My words are true, and now must thou keep the vow by which thou didst swear to love me, if Procris should yield herself to a stranger.' So Kephalos dwelt with Eôs; but for all her fond words he could not love her as still he loved Procris.

Meanwhile Procris wandered, in deep and bitter sorrow, among the hills and valleys of Crete. She cared not to look on the fair morning as it broke on the pale path of night; she cared not to watch the bright sun as he rose from the dark sea, or when he sank to rest behind the western waters. For her the earth had lost all its gladness, and she felt that she could die. But one day, as she sat on a hillside and looked on the broad plains which lay stretched beneath, suddenly a woman stood before her, brighter and more glorious than the daughters of men; and Procris knew, from the spear which she held in her hand and the hound which crouched before her, that it was Artemis, the mighty child of Zeus and Leto. Then Procris fell at her feet, and said, 'O Lady Artemis, pity me in my great sorrow;' and Artemis answered, 'Fear not, Procris; I know thy grief. Kephalos hath done thee a great wrong, but he shall fall by the same device wherewith he requited thy pure and trusting love.' So she gave to Procris her hound and her spear, and said, 'Hasten now to thine own land; and go stand before Kephalos, and I will put a spell upon him, that he may not know thee. Follow him in the chase; and at whatsoever thou mayest cast this spear, it shall fall, and from this hound no prey which thou mayest seek for shall ever escape.'

So Procris sailed back to the land of Erectheus with the gifts of Artemis. And when Kephalos went to the chase, Procris followed him; and all the glory of the hunt fell to her portion, for the hound struck down whatever it seized, and her spear never missed its aim. And Kephalos marvelled greatly, and said to the maiden, 'Give me thy hound and thy spear;' and he besought the stranger many times for the gift, till at last Procris said, 'I will not give them but for thy love; thou must forsake Eôs and come to dwell with me.' Then Kephalos said, 'I care not for Eôs; so only I have thy gifts, thou shalt have my love.' But even as he spake these words, a change came over the face of the stranger, and he saw that it was Procris herself who stood before him. And Procris said, 'Ah, Kephalos, once more thou hast promised to love me; and now may I keep thy love, and remain with thee always. Almost I may say that I never loved any one but thee; but thou art changed, Kephalos, although still the same; else wouldst thou not have promised to love me for the gift of a hound and a spear.' Then Kephalos besought Procris to forgive him, and he said, 'I am caught in the trap which I laid for thee; but I have fallen deeper. When thou gavest thy love to me as to a stranger, it pleased thee yet to think that I was like Kephalos; and now my vow to thee has been given for the mere gifts which I coveted.' But Procris only said, 'My joy is come back to me again, and now will I leave thee no more.'

So once more, in the land of Erectheus, Procris and Kephalos dwelt together in a true and a deep love. Once more they wandered over hill and dale as in the times that were past, and looked out from the heights of Hymettos to the white shore of Eubœa, as it glistened in the light of early day. But whenever he went to the chase with the hound and the spear of Artemis, Procris saw that Eôs still watched if haply she might talk with Kephalos alone, and win him again for herself. Once more she was happy, but her happiness was not what it had been when Kephalos first gave her his love, while her father Erectheus was yet alive. She knew that Eôs still envied her, and she sought to guard Kephalos from the danger of her treacherous look and enticing words. So she kept ever near him in the chase, although he saw her not; and thus it came to pass that one day, as Procris watched him from a thicket, the folds of her dress rustled against the branches, so that Kephalos thought it was some beast moving from its den, and hurled at her the spear of Artemis that never missed its mark. Then he heard the cry as of one who has received a deadly blow, and when he hastened into the thicket, Procris lay smitten down to the earth before him. The coldness of death was on her face, and her bright eye was dim; but her voice was as loving as ever, while she said, 'O Kephalos, it grieves me not that thy arm hath struck me down. I have thy love; and having it, I go to the land of the bright heroes, where my father Erectheus is waiting for his child, and where thou too shalt one day meet me, to dwell with me for ever.' One loving look she gave to Kephalos, and the smile of parting vanished in the stillness of death.

Then over the body of Procris Kephalos wept tears of bitter sorrow; and he said, 'Ah, Eôs, Eôs, well hast thou rewarded me for doubting once a love such as thou couldst never feel.' Many days and many weeks he mourned for his lost love; and daily he sat on the slopes of Hymettos, and thought with a calm and almost happy grief how Procris there had rested by his side. All this time the spear of Artemis was idle, and the hound went not forth to the chase, until chieftains came from other lands to ask his aid against savage beasts or men. Among them came Amphitryon, the lord of Thebes, to ask for help; and Kephalos said, 'I will do as thou wouldst have me. It is time that I should begin to journey to the bright land where Procris dwells beyond the western sea.'

So he went with Amphitryon into the Theban land, and hunted out the savage beasts which wasted his harvests; and then he journeyed on till he came to the home of Phœbus Apollo at Delphi. There the god bade him hasten to the

western sea, where he should once again find
Procris. Onward he went, across the heights
and vales of Ætolia, until at last he stood on
the Leucadian cape[7] and looked out on the blue
waters. The sun was sinking low down in the
sky, and the golden clouds of evening were
gathered round him as he hastened to his rest.
And Kephalos said, 'Here must I rest also, for
my journey is done, and Procris is waiting for
me in the brighter land.'[8] There on the white
cliff he stood, and just as the sun touched the
waters, the strength of Kephalos failed him, and
he sank gently into the sea.

So again, in the homes of the bright heroes,
Kephalos found the wife whom he had loved and
slain.

THE VALE OF THE PENKIOI

DAPHNÊ.

IN the vale of Tempê, where the stream of Peneios flows beneath the heights of Olympus towards the sea, the beautiful Daphnê passed the days of her happy childhood. Fresh as the earliest morning, she climbed the crags to greet the first rays of the rising sun; and when he had driven his fiery horses over the sky, she watched his chariot sink behind the western hills. Over hill and dale she roamed, free and light as the breeze of spring. Other maidens round her spoke each of her love, but Daphnê cared not to listen to the voice of man, though many a one sought her to be his wife.

One day, as she stood on the slopes of Ossa in the glow of early morning, she saw before her a glorious form. The light of the new-risen sun fell on his face with a golden splendour, and she knew that it was Phœbus Apollo. Hastily he ran towards her, and said, 'O maiden, child of the morning, I have found thee. Others thou hast cast aside, but from me thou canst not

escape. I have sought thee long, and now will
I make thee mine.' But the heart of Daphnê
was bold and strong; and her cheek flushed and
her eye sparkled with anger, as she said, 'I know
neither love nor bondage. I live free among the
streams and hills; and to none will I yield my
freedom.' Then the face of Apollo grew dark
with anger, and he drew near to seize the maiden;
but swift as the wind she fled away. Over hill
and dale, over crag and river, the feet of Daphnê
fell lightly as falling leaves in autumn; but
nearer yet came Phœbus Apollo, till at last the
strength of the maiden began to fail. Then she
stretched out her hands, and cried for help to the
Lady Dêmêtêr; but she came not to her aid.
Her head was dizzy, and her limbs trembled in
utter feebleness as she drew near to the broad
river which gladdens the plains of Thessaly, till
she almost felt the breath of Phœbus and her
robe was almost in his grasp. Then, with a wild
cry, she said, 'O father Peneios, receive thy child,'
and she rushed into the stream, whose waters
closed gently over her.

She was gone; and Apollo mourned for his
madness in chasing thus the free maiden. And
he said, 'I have punished myself by my folly;
the light of the morning is taken out of the day.

I must go on alone till my journey shall draw towards its end.'⁹ Then he spake the word, and a laurel came up on the bank where Daphnê had plunged into the stream; and the green bush with its thick clustering leaves keeps her name for ever.

THE DELIAN APOLLO.

FROM land to land the Lady Leto wandered in fear and sorrow, for no city or country would give her a home where she might abide in peace. From Crete to Athens, from Athens to Ægina, from Ægina to the heights of Pelion and Athos, through all the islands of the wide Ægæan Sea, Skyros and Imbros and Lemnos, and Chios the fairest of all, she passed, seeking a home. But in vain she prayed each land to receive her, until she came to the island of Delos, and promised to raise it to great glory if only there she might rest in peace. And she lifted up her voice and said, 'Listen to me, O island of the dark sea: if thou wilt grant me a home, all nations shall come unto thee, and great wealth shall flow in upon thee; for here shall Phœbus Apollo, the lord of light and life, be born, and men shall come hither to know his will and win his favour.' Then answered Delos and said, ' O lady, thou promisest great things; but they say that the power of Phœbus Apollo will be such as nothing

on the wide earth may withstand; and mine is
but a poor and stony soil, where there is little to
please the eye of those who look upon me. Wherefore I fear that he will despise my hard and
barren land, and go to some other country where
he will build a more glorious temple, and grant
richer gifts to the people who come to worship
him.' But Leto sware by the dark water of Styx,
and the wide heaven above, and the broad earth
around her, that in Delos should be the shrine
of Phœbus, and that there should the rich offerings burn on his altar the whole year round.

So Leto rested in the island of Delos, and there
was Phœbus Apollo born. And there was joy
among the undying gods who dwell in Olympus,
and the earth laughed beneath the smile of
heaven. Then was his temple built in Delos, and
men came to it from all lands to learn his will
and offer rich sacrifices on his altar.[10]

THE PYTHIAN APOLLO.

LONG time Apollo abode in Delos; and every year all the children of Iôn were gathered to the feast which was held before his temple. But at length it came to pass that Apollo went through many lands, journeying towards Pytho. With harp in hand he drew nigh to the gates of Olympus where Zeus and the gods dwell in their glory; and straightway all rejoiced for the sweetness of his harping. The Muses sang the undying gifts of the gods, and the griefs and woes of mortal men who cannot flee from old age and death. The bright Horæ joined hands together with Hebe and Harmonia; and Ares stood by the side of Aphroditê with Hermes the slayer of Argus, gazing on the face of Phœbus Apollo which glistened as with the light of the new-risen sun. Then from Olympus he went down into the Pierian land, to Iolcos and the Lelantian plain; but it pleased him not there to build himself a home. Thence he wandered on to Mycalessus, and, traversing the grassy plains of Teumessus, came to the sacred Thebes; but neither would he dwell there, for no man had yet come thither, neither was there road or path but only wild forest in all the land.

Further and further he roamed, across the stream of Kephisos and beyond Ocalea and Haliartos, until he came to Telphûsa. There he thought to build himself a temple, for the land was rich and fair; so he said, 'O Telphûsa¹¹, here would I rest in thy happy vale, and here shall men come to ask my will and seek for aid in the hour of fear; and great glory shall come to thee while I abide in thy land.' But Telphûsa was moved with anger as she saw Phœbus marking out the place for his shrine and laying its foundations; and she spake craftily to him and said, 'Listen to me, Phœbus Apollo. Thou seekest here to have a home, but here thou canst never rest in peace; for my broad plain will tempt men to the strife of battle, and the tramp of warhorses shall vex the stillness of thy holy temple. Nay, even in time of peace, the lowing cattle shall come in crowds to my fountain, and the tumult shall grieve thine heart. But go thou to Crisa, and make for thyself a home in the hidden clefts of Parnassus, and thither shall men hasten with their gifts from the utmost bounds of the earth.' So Apollo believed her words, and he went on through the land of the Phlegyes until he came to Crisa. There he laid the foundations of his shrine in the deep cleft of Parnassus; and Trophonios and Agamedes, the children of Erginos, raised the walls. There also he found the mighty dragon who nursed Typhaon, the child of Hêrê, and he smote him and said, 'Rot there upon the ground, and vex not more the children of men. The days of thy life are ended, neither can Typhöeus himself aid thee now, or Chimæra of the evil name. But the earth and the burning sun shall consume and scorch thy body.' So the dragon died, and his body rotted on the ground; wherefore the name of that place is called Pytho, and they worship Phœbus Apollo as the great Pythian king.

But Phœbus knew now that Telphûsa had deceived him, because she said nothing of the great dragon of Crisa, or of the roughness of the land. So he hastened back in his anger and said, 'O Telphûsa, thou hast beguiled me with thy crafty words; but no more shall thy fountain send forth its sweet water, and the glory shall be mine alone.' So Apollo hurled great crags down and choked the stream near the beautiful fountain, and the glory departed from Telphûsa.

Then he thought within himself what men he should choose to be his priests at Pytho; and far away, as he stood on a high hill, he saw a ship sailing on the wine-faced sea, and the men who were in it were Cretans, sailing from the land of King Minos to barter their goods with the men of Pylos. So Phœbus leaped into the sea and changed his form to the form of a dolphin, and hastened to meet the ship. None knew whence the great fish came which smote the side of their vessel with its mighty fins; but all marvelled at the sight, as the dolphin guided the ship through the dark waters. So they sat trembling with fear, as they sped on without a sail by the force of the strong south wind. From the headland of Malea and the land of the Laconians they passed to Helos and to Tænaron where Helios dwells in whom the sons of men take delight, and where his cattle feed in the rich pastures.'² There the sailors would have ended their wanderings; but they sought in vain to land, for the ship would not obey its helm. Onward it went along the coasts of the island of Pelops, for the mighty dolphin guided it. So from Arênê and Arguphea it came to the sandy Pylos, by Chalkis and Dymê to the land of the Epeians, to Pheræ and to Ithaca. There the men saw spread out before them the waters which wash the shores of Crisa; and the strong west wind came with its fierce breath, and drove them on to the east and towards the sunrising, until they came to Crisa.

Then Phœbus Apollo came forth from the sea like a star, and the brightness of his glory reached up to the high heaven. Into his shrine he hastened, and on the altar he kindled the undying fire, and his bright arrows were hurled abroad, till all Crisa was filled with the blaze of his lightnings, so that fear came upon all, and the cries of the women rose shrill in the sultry air. Then, swift as a thought of the heart, he hastened back to the ship; but his form was now the form of a man in his beauty, and his golden locks flowed down over his broad shoulders. From the shore he called out to the men in the Cretan ship, and said, 'Who are ye, strangers, and do ye come as thieves and robbers, bringing terror and sorrow whithersoever ye may go? Why stay ye thus, tarrying in your ship, and seek not to come out upon the land? Surely ye must know that all who sail on the wide sea rejoice when their ship comes to the shore, that so they may come forth and feast with the people of the land.' So spake Phœbus Apollo; and the

leader of the Cretans took courage and said,
'O stranger, sure I am that thou art no mortal
man, but one of the bright heroes or the undying
gods. Wherefore tell us now the name of this
land and of the people who dwell in it. Hither
we never sought to come, for we were sailing
from the land of Minos to barter our wares at
Pylos; but some one of the gods hath brought
us hither against our will.' Then spake the
mighty Apollo and said to them, 'O strangers,
who have dwelt in Knossos of the Cretan land,
think not to return to your ancient home, to
your wives or to your children; but here ye
must guard and keep my shrine, and ye shall be
honoured of all the children of men. For I am
the son of Zeus, and my name is Phœbus Apollo.
It was I who brought you hither across the wide
sea, not in guile or anger, but that in all time to
come ye may have great power and glory, that
ye may learn the counsels of the undying gods
and make known their will to men. Hasten
then to do my bidding; let down your sails, and
bring your ship to the shore. Then bring out
your goods and build an altar on the beach, and
kindle a fire and offer white barley as an offering; and because I led you hither under the
form of a dolphin, so worship me as the Delphian

god. Then eat bread and drink wine, as much as your soul may lust after; and after that come with me to the holy place where ye shall guard my temple.'

So they obeyed the words of Phœbus; and when they had offered the white barley and feasted richly on the sea-shore, they rose up to go; and Apollo led them on their way. His harp was in his hand, and he made sweet music, such as no mortal ear had ever heard before; and they raised the chant of Io Pæan, for a new power was breathed into their hearts, as they went along. They thought not now of toil or sorrow; but with feet unwearied they went up the hill until they reached the clefts of Parnassus, where Phœbus would have them dwell.

Then out spake the leader of the Cretans and said boldly, 'O king, thou hast brought us far away from our homes to a strange land; whence are we to get food here? No harvests will grow on these bare rocks, no meadows are spread out before our eyes. The whole land is bare and desolate.' But the son of Zeus smiled and said, 'O foolish men, and easy to be cast down, if ye had your wish ye would gain nothing but care and toil. But listen to me and ponder well my words. Stretch forth your hands, and slay each day the rich offerings, for they shall come to you without stint and sparing, seeing that the sons of men shall hasten hither from all lands, to learn my will and ask for aid in the hour of fear. Only guard ye my temple well, and keep your hands clean and your heart pure: for if ye deal rightly no man shall take away your glory; but if ye speak lies and do iniquity, if ye hurt the people who come to my altar, and make them to go astray, then shall other men rise up in your place, and ye yourselves shall be thrust out for ever, because ye would not obey my words.'[13]

THE VENGEANCE OF APOLLO.[14]

IN the cool evening time King Darius walked in his royal garden, and the noblest of the Persians were around him. Then came there a messenger from the western land in haste and said, 'O King, the men of Athens with the sons of Javan have taken thy city of Sardes, and the temple of the great goddess Kybêbê has been burnt.' And King Darius answered quickly and said, 'What sayest thou, O messenger, that men of whose name I never heard have come with my slaves against the land of the great king?' Then he bade them bring a bow and arrows; and while one went for them, the Persians stood round him in silence, for they feared to say aught while the king was angry. So when he took the bow, he fitted an arrow to it and shot it up into the sky, and prayed, saying, 'O Zeus, that dwellest in the high heavens, suffer me to be avenged upon the men of Athens. The sons of Javan are my slaves, and sorely shall they be smitten for the deeds which they have

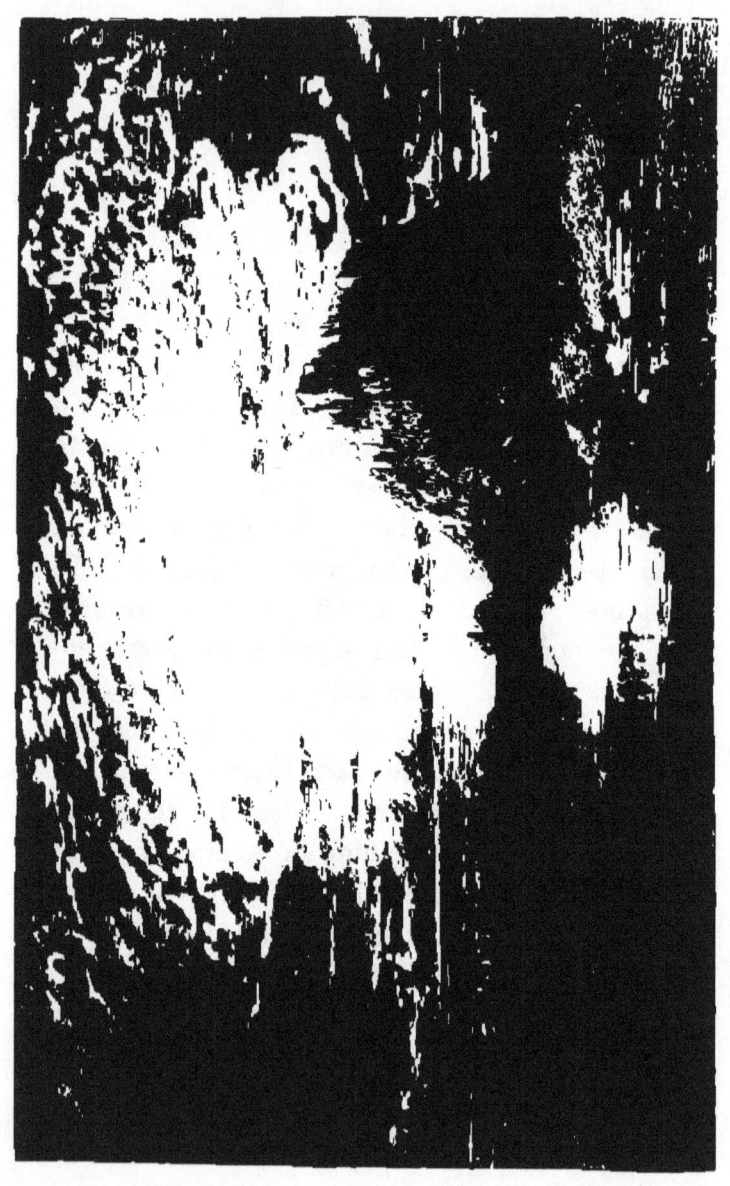

done.' Then he gave command, and each day, when the banquet was spread in the gilded hall, and the king sat down to meat, there stood forth one who said with a loud voice, 'O king, forget not the men of Athens.'

But Zeus hearkened not to the prayer of the great king, for the ships were made ready, and his chieftains and warriors hastened away to the Athenian land, and fought in Marnthon. But they fared not well in the battle, for the men of Athens strove mightily for their country, and the bright heroes came back to aid their kinsfolk. Then were there seen wonderful forms taller and more glorious than the sons of men; and the mighty Echetlæos with his great ploughshare smote down the chiefest of the Medes. So in great fear the Persians fled to the sea-shore, while the men of Athens slew them on the land and in the water as they struggled to reach the ships. And when the fight was over, they spoiled the Persians who lay dead on the sea-shore, and took rich plunder, for scattered about they found embroidered turbans and bright swords and daggers, and golden bits and bridles, and silken robes and jewels.

Thus sped the hosts of King Darius; and the messenger came again in his haste, as he sat on his golden throne in Susa, while the nobles of Persia did obeisance before him. Then the king said, 'Speak, O man, hast thou brought good tidings that my slaves have chastised the people of the strange city?' And the messenger answered, saying, 'O king, the men of Athens have slain thy mighty men with the sword, and burnt thy ships; and few have come back of all the great army which thou didst send against them.'

Great and fierce was the wrath of King Darius when he heard the tidings, and he hastened to make ready ships and men and horses, that he might go forth himself against the men of Athens. Then in every city of the Persian land was heard the din as of men who have a great work to do; and the armourers wrought spears and swords and shields, and in the harbours they built countless ships to sail over the dark sea. But Zeus hearkened not yet to the prayer of the king; so Darius died, and Xerxes his son sat upon his throne, and the chief men of the Persians were gathered round him. Then the king spake and said, 'Be ready, O Persians, every one of you, for I will go forth with all my great power, and make slaves of the men of Athens; and so may the gods do to me, and more also, if I burn not the temples of their gods with fire, and bring not hither the golden treasures which lie in the house of Phœbus Apollo at Delphi.'

Then, with all his great hosts, King Xerxes set forth from Susa, and his satraps and warriors and slaves followed him, with a great multitude of every nation and people; and they crossed over from the land of Asia by a bridge which was built over the sea of Hellê. Then they journeyed on in pomp and glory, and King Xerxes thought that they had done great things when his hosts slew Leonidas and three hundred men of Sparta who guarded the passes of Thermopylæ. So his heart was filled with pride, and he chose out the bravest of his warriors, and charged the men of Thessaly to lead them to Delphi and the temple of Phœbus Apollo.

Then was there great fear and terror in Delphi, for a messenger came and said, 'The hosts of King Xerxes are coming to slay the men of this land and take away the treasures which lie in the house of King Apollo.' So they went in great sorrow to the temple, and bowed their heads to the earth and prayed, saying, 'O child of the light, who dwellest here in thy holy temple, thieves and robbers are coming against us, and they are purposed to take away thy sacred treasures; tell us, then, what we shall do, for at thy bidding we are ready to bury them deep in the earth till the storm of war be overpast.' Then came there a voice from the inmost shrine, but it was not the voice of the priestess, for Phœbus Apollo himself came down to speak his will, and said, 'Move them not, O men of Delphi. I will guard my holy place, and none shall lay hand on my sacred things.'

So they went away in gladness of heart, and made ready for the coming of the Persians; and all the men of Delphi left the city, saving only sixty men and the prophet Akeratos, and these sat down before the steps of the temple. In silence they waited till the Persians should come; and they marvelled at the great stillness on the earth and in the heaven. There was not a cloud in the sky, and the two peaks of Parnassus glistened in the blazing sunshine. Not a breath lifted the green leaves of the sacred laurels, not a bird sang in the breathless air. Presently, as he turned round to look, the prophet saw the sacred weapons of Phœbus, which no mortal man might touch, lying on the temple steps; and he said to the sixty men who tarried with him, 'Lo, now will Phœbus fight for his holy temple, for his own hand hath made ready the weapons for the battle.'

Soon in the deep valley and along the bank of the Castalian stream were seen the hosts of the Persians, as they came on with their long spears flashing in the bright sunshine. Far away the men of Delphi saw the blaze of their burnished armour, and heard the tramp of their warhorses. Onward they came, and they said one to another, 'The gods have fought for us, and the prize is won already. See, yonder is the home of Phœbus, and none remain of the men of Delphi to do battle for his holy temple.'

So still the sun shone without a cloud in the sky, and no breeze broke the stillness of the laurel groves. Still glistened the sacred arms as they lay on the steps of the temple, and the opened doors showed the golden treasures which were stored up within. There lay the throne of Midas, and the golden lion of Crœsus. There lay the mighty mixing bowl, all of pure gold, which, at the bidding of Crœsus, was wrought by the Samian Theodoros. There lay all the rich gifts which the men of Hellas had offered up to win the favour of the Lord Apollo.

Then the leaders of the Persians stretched forth their hands, as though all these things were given up to them by the god who had forsaken his people; but even as they came near to his holy ground, the lightning flashed forth, and the crash of the thunder was heard in the blue heaven, and the dark cloud fell on the peaks of Parnassus. Then, like the roar of a raging torrent, burst forth the mighty wind. Down from the steeps of the Delphian hill thundered the huge rocks, and trees uptorn from their roots were hurled on the hosts of the barbarians. Louder and fiercer grew the din; and cries and shoutings were heard from the Alean chapel, for the virgin Athênê fought against the men of Xerxes. Smitten by the fiery lightnings, they fell on the quaking earth, when suddenly there was heard a sound more fierce and terrible, and two cliffs were hurled down from the mountain-top. Underneath this huge mass the mightiest of the Persians lay still in the sleep of death; and all who yet lived fled with quaking hearts and trembling steps from the great wrath of Phœbus.

So fought the god for his holy temple; and when from their hiding-places the men of Delphi saw that the Persians fled, then from caves and thickets they poured forth to slay them; and they smote them even as sheep are slain before the altar of sacrifice, for even the bravest of their

warriors lifted not their arm against them. Long
time they followed after them in hot haste; and
among them were seen two giant forms, clothed
in bright armour, smiting down the hosts of
the enemy. Then they knew that Phylacos and
Autonoös, the heroes of the place, had come forth
to aid them, and they smote the Persians more
fiercely till the going down of the sun.

So the fight was ended; and the stars came forth
in the cloudless sky, and the laurel groves were
stirred by the soft evening breeze. With songs
of high thanksgiving the men of Delphi drew
near to the temple, and they saw that Phœbus
had placed again within his shrine the sacred
arms which no mortal man may handle. Then
was there rich spoil gathered, and the holy place of
Apollo shone with gifts of gold and silver, which
the men of Delphi offered in gladness of heart for
all the great things which he had done for them.
And in every house of the Delphians were seen
robes and turbans rich with gold and silver and
embroidery. On their walls hung spears and
shields, and swords and daggers, which the Persians bore when they came to Delphi.

So in after days they told their children the
wondrous tale how Phœbus Apollo smote down

the hosts of Xerxes; and they showed them the spoils which they took by the aid of the bright heroes, and the two rocks, lying on the holy ground before his shrine, which Phœbus tore from the peaks of Parnassus in the day of his great vengeance.

THE TOILS OF HERACLES.

BY the doom of his father Zeus, Heracles served in Argos the false and cruel Eurystheus. For so it was that Zeus spake of the birth of Heracles to Hêrê, the queen, and said, 'This day shall a child be born of the race of Perseus, who shall be the mightiest of the sons of men.' Even so he spake, because Atê had deceived him by her evil counsel. And Hêrê asked whether this should be so in very deed; and Zeus bowed his head, and the word went forth which could not be recalled. Then Hêrê went to the mighty Eileithuiæ, and by their aid she brought it about that Eurystheus was born before Heracles the son of Zeus.

So the lot was fixed that all his life long Heracles should toil at the will of a weak and crafty master. Brave in heart and stout of body, so that no man might be matched with him for strength or beauty, yet was he to have no profit of all his labour till he should come to the land of the undying gods. For it grieved Zeus that the craft of Hêrê, the queen, had brought grievous wrong on his child, and he cast forth Atê from the halls of Olympus, that she might no more dwell among the gods.[15] Then he spake the word that Heracles should dwell with the gods in Olympus, as soon as the days of his toil on earth should be ended.

Thus the child grew in the house of Amphitryon, full of beauty and might, so that men marvelled at his great strength; for as he lay one day sleeping, there came two serpents into the chamber, and twisted their long coils round the cradle, and peered upon him with their cold glassy eyes, till the sound of their hissing woke him from his slumber. But Heracles trembled not for fear, but stretched forth his arms and placed his hands on the serpents' necks, and tightened his grasp more and more till they fell dead on the ground. Then all knew by this sign that Heracles must do great things and suffer many sorrows, but that in the end he should win the victory. So the child waxed great and strong, and none could be matched with him for strength of arm and swiftness of foot and in taming of horses and in wrestling. The best men in Argos were his teachers, and the wise centaur Cheiron was his friend and taught him ever to help the weak and take their part against any who oppressed them. So, for all his great strength, none were more gentle than Heracles, none more full of pity for those who were bowed down by pain and labour.

But it was a sore grief to Heracles that all his life long he must toil for Eurystheus, while others were full of joy and pleasure and feasted at tables laden with good things. And so it came to pass that one day, as he thought of these things, he sat down by the wayside, where two paths met, in a lonely valley far away from the dwellings of men.[16] Suddenly, as he lifted up his eyes, he saw two women coming towards him, each from a different road. They were both fair to look upon; but the one had a soft and gentle face, and she was clad in a seemly robe of pure white. The other looked boldly at Heracles, and her face was more ruddy, and her eyes shone with a hot and restless light. From her shoulders streamed the long folds of her soft embroidered robe, which scantly hid the beauty of her form beneath. With a quick and eager step she hastened to Heracles, that so she might be the first to speak. And she said, 'I know, O man of much toil and sorrow, that thy heart is sad within thee, and that thou knowest not which way thou shalt turn. Come then with me, and I will lead thee on a soft and pleasant road, where no storms shall vex thee and no sorrows shall trouble thee. Thou shalt never hear of wars and battles, and sickness and pain shall not come nigh to thee. But all day long shalt thou feast at rich banquets and listen to the songs of minstrels. Thou shalt not want for sparkling wine, and soft robes, and pleasant couches; thou shalt not lack the delights of love, for the bright eyes of maidens shall look gently upon thee, and their song shall lull thee to sleep in the soft evening hour, when the stars come out in the sky.' And Heracles said, 'Thou promisest to me pleasant things, O lady, and I am sorely pressed down by a hard master. What is thy name?' 'My friends,' she said, 'call me the happy and joyous one; but they who look not upon me with love have given me an evil name, but they speak falsely.'

Then the other spake and said, 'O Heracles, I too know whence thou art, and the doom that is laid upon thee, and how thou hast lived and toiled even from the days of thy childhood; and therefore I think that thou wilt give me thy love, and if thou dost, then men shall speak of thy good deeds in time to come, and my name shall be yet more exalted. But I have no fair words wherewith to cheat thee. Nothing good is ever reached without labour; nothing great is ever won without toil. If thou seek for fruit from the earth, thou must tend and till it; if thou wouldst have the favour of the undying gods, thou must come before them with prayers and offerings; if thou longest for the love of men, thou must do them good.' Then the other brake in upon her words and said, 'O Heracles, thou seest that Aretê seeks to lead thee on a long and weary path, but my broad and easy road leads thee quickly to happiness.' But Aretê answered her (and her eye flashed with anger), 'O wretched one, what good thing hast thou to give, and what pleasure canst thou feel, who knowest not what it is to toil? Thy lusts are pampered, thy taste is dull. Thou quaffest the rich wine before thou art thirsty, and fillest thyself with dainties before thou art hungry. Though thou art numbered amongst the undying ones, the gods have cast thee forth out of heaven, and good men scorn thee. The sweetest of all sounds, when a man's heart praises him, thou hast never heard; the sweetest of all sights, when a man looks on his good deeds, thou hast never seen. They who bow down to thee are weak and feeble in youth, and wretched and loathsome in old age. But I dwell with the gods in heaven, and with good men on the earth; and without me nothing good and pure may be

thought and done. More than all others am I
honoured by the gods, more than all others am I
cherished by the men who love me. In peace
and in war, in health and in sickness, I am the
aid of all who seek me; and my help never fails.
My children know the purest of all pleasures, when
the hour of rest comes after the toil of day. In
youth they are strong, and their limbs are quick
with health; in old age they look back upon a
happy life, and when they lie down to the sleep
of death, their name is cherished among men for
their brave and good deeds. Love me, therefore, O Heracles, and obey my words, and thou
shalt dwell with me, when thy toil is ended, in
the home of the undying gods.'

Then Heracles bowed down his head, and sware
to follow her counsels; and when the two maidens
passed away from his sight, he went forth with a
good courage to his labour and suffering. In many
a land he sojourned and toiled to do the will of
the false Eurystheus. Good deeds he did for the
sons of men; but he had no profit of all his labour,
save the love of the gentle Iolê. Far away in
Œchalia, where the sun rises from the eastern
sea, he saw the maiden in the halls of Eurytos,
and sought to win her love. But the word which
Zeus spake to Hêrê the queen, gave him no rest;

and Eurystheus sent him forth to other lands, and he saw the maiden no more.

But Heracles toiled on with a good heart, and soon the glory of his great deeds was spread abroad throughout all the earth. Minstrels sang how Heracles slew the monsters and savage beasts who vexed the sons of men, how he smote the Hydra in the land of Lernæ, and the wild boar which haunted the groves of Erymanthos, and the Harpies who lurked in the swamps of Stymphalos. They told how he wandered far away to the land of the setting sun, when Eurystheus bade him pluck the golden apples from the garden of the Hesperides,—how over hill and dale, across marsh and river, through thicket and forest, he came to the western sea, and crossed to the African land where Atlas lifts up his white head to the high heaven,—how he smote the dragon which guarded the brazen gates, and brought the apples to King Eurystheus. They sang of his weary journey when he roamed through the land of the Ethiopians and came to the wild and desolate heights of Caucasus,— how he saw a giant form high on the naked rock, and the vulture which gnawed the Titan's heart with its beak. They told how he slew the bird, and smote off the cruel chains, and set Prometheus free. They sang how Eurystheus laid on him a fruitless task and sent him down to the dark land of King Hades to bring up the monster Kerberos, how upon the shore of the gloomy Acheron he found the mighty hound who guards the home of Hades and Persephone, how he seized him in his strong right hand and bare him to King Eurystheus.[17] They sang of the days when he toiled in the land of Queen Omphalê beneath the Lydian sun, how he destroyed the walls of Ilion when Laomedon was king, and how he went to Calydon and wooed and won Dêianeira, the daughter of the chieftain Œneus.

Long time he abode in Calydon, and the people of the land loved him for his kindly deeds. But one day his spear smote the boy Eunomos; and his father was not angry, because he knew that Heracles sought not to slay him. Yet Heracles would go forth from the land, for his heart was grieved for the death of the child. So he journeyed to the banks of the Evênos, where he smote the centaur Nessos because he sought to lay hands on Dêianeira. Swiftly the poison from the barb of the spear ran through his veins; but Nessos knew how to avenge himself on Heracles, and with a faint voice he besought her to fill a shell with his blood, so that, if ever she lost the love of Heracles, she might win it again by spreading it on a robe for him to wear.

So Nessos died; and Heracles went to the land of Trachis, and there Dêianeira abode while he journeyed to the eastern sea. Many times the moon waxed and waned in the heaven, and the corn sprang up from the ground and gave its golden harvest; but Heracles came not back. At last the tidings came how he had done great deeds in distant lands, how Eurytos the king of Œchalia was slain, and how among the captives was the daughter of the king, the fairest of all the maidens of the land.

Then the words of Nessos came back to Dêianeira, and she hastened to anoint a broidered robe; for she thought only that the love of Heracles had passed away from her, and that she must win it to herself again. So, with words of love and honour, she sent the gift for Heracles to put on; and the messenger found him on the Keneian shore where he was offering rich sacrifice to Zeus his father, and gave him the broidered robe in token of the love of Dêianiera. Then Heracles wrapped it closely round him, and he stood by the altar while the dark smoke went up in a thick cloud to the heaven. Presently the vengeance of Nessos was accomplished. Through the veins of Heracles the poison spread like devouring fire. Fiercer and fiercer grew the burning pain, and Heracles strove vainly to tear the robe and cast it from him. It ate into his flesh; and as he struggled in his agony, the dark blood gushed from his body in streams. Then came the maiden Iolê to his side. With her gentle hands she sought to soothe his pain, and with pitying words to cheer him in his woe. Then once more the face of Heracles flushed with a deep joy, and his eye glanced with a pure light, as in the days of his might and strength; and he said, 'Ah, Iolê, brightest of maidens, thy voice shall cheer me as I sink down in the sleep of death. I loved thee in the bright morning time, when my hand was strong and my foot swift; but Zeus willed not that thou shouldst be with me in my long wanderings. Yet I grieve not now, for again thou hast come, fair as the soft clouds which gather round the dying sun.' Then Heracles bade them bear him to the high crest of Œta and gather wood. So, when all was ready, he lay down to rest, and they kindled the great pile. The black mists were spreading over the sky, but still Heracles sought to gaze on the fair face of Iolê and to comfort her in her sorrow. 'Weep not, Iolê,' he said; 'my toil is done, and now is the time for rest. I shall see thee again in the bright land which is never trodden by the feet of night.'

Blacker and blacker grew the evening shades; and only the long line of light broke the darkness which gathered round the blazing pile. Then from the high heaven came down the thick cloud, and the din of its thunder crashed through the air. So Zeus carried his child home, and the halls of Olympus were opened to welcome the bright hero who rested from his mighty toil. There the fair maiden Areté placed a crown upon his head, and Hébé clothed him in a white robe for the banquet of the gods.[18]

ALTHÆA AND THE BURNING BRAND.

THERE was feasting in the halls of Œneus the chieftain of Calydôn in the Ætolian land, and all prayed for wealth and glory for the chief, and for his wife Althæa, and for the child who had on that day been born to them. And Œneus besought the king of gods and men with rich offerings, that his son Meleagros might win a name greater than his own, that he might grow up stout of heart and strong of arm, and that in time to come men might say, 'Meleagros wrought mighty works and did good deeds to the people of the land.'

But the mighty Mœræ, whose word even Zeus himself may not turn aside, had fixed the doom of Meleagros.[19] The child lay sleeping in his mother's arms, and Althæa prayed that her son might grow up brave and gentle, and be to her a comforter in the time of age and the hour of death. Suddenly, as she yet spake, the Mœræ stood before her. There was no love or pity in their cold grey eye, and they looked down with stern unchanging faces on the mother and her child, and one of them said, 'The brand burns on the hearth: when it is burnt wholly, thy child shall die.' But love is swifter than thought; and the mother snatched the burning brand from the fire, and quenched its flame in water; and she placed it in a secret place where no hand but her own might reach it.

So the child grew, brave of heart and sturdy of limb, and ever ready to hunt the wild beasts or to go against the cities of men. Many great deeds he did in the far-off Colchian land, when the chieftains sailed with Athamas and Ino to take away the golden fleece from King Æêtês.[20] But there were greater things for him to do when he came again to Calydon, for his father Œneus had roused the wrath of the mighty Artemis. There was rich banqueting in his great hall, when his harvest was ingathered; and Zeus and all the other gods feasted on the fat burnt-offerings; but no gift was set apart for the virgin child of Lêto. Soon she requited the wrong to Œneus, and a savage boar was seen in the land, which tare up the fruit-trees, and destroyed the seed in the ground, and trampled on the green corn as it came up. None dared to approach it, for its mighty tusks tare everything that crossed its path. Long time the chieftains took counsel what they should do, until Meleagros said, 'I will go forth: who will follow me?' Then from Calydon and from the cities and lands round about came mighty chieftains and brave youths, even as they had hastened to the ship Argo when they sought to win the golden fleece from Colchis. With them came the Curêtes who live in Pleurôn, and among them were seen Castor and Polydeukês the twin brethren, and Theseus with his comrade Peirithoös, and Jason and Admetos. But more beautiful than all was Atalantê, the daughter of Schœneus, a stranger from the Arcadian land. Much the chieftains sought to keep her from the chase, for the maiden's arm was strong, and her feet swift, and her aim sure; and they liked not that she should come from a far country to share their glory or take away their name. But Meleagros loved the fair and brave maiden; and he said, 'If she go not to the chase, neither will I go with you.' So they suffered her, and the chase began. At first the boar fled, trampling down those whom he chanced to meet, and rending them with his tusks; but at length he stood fiercely at bay, and fought furiously, and many of the hunters fell, until at length the spear of

Atalantê pierced his side, and then Meleagros slew him.

Then was there great gladness, as they dragged the body of the boar to Calydon, and made ready to divide the spoil. But the anger of Artemis was not yet soothed; and she roused a strife between the men of Pleuron and the men of Calydon. For Meleagros sought to have the head, and the Curêtes of Pleuron cared not to take the hide only for their portion. So the strife grew hot between them, until Meleagros slew the chieftain of the Curêtes, who was the brother of Althæa his mother. Then he seized the head of the boar, and bare it to Atalantê, and said, 'Take, O maiden, the spoils that are rightly thine. From thy spear came the first wound which smote down the boar; and well hast thou earned the prize for the fleetness of thy foot and the sureness of thy aim.'

So Atalantê took the spoils and carried them to her home in the Arcadian land; but the men of Pleuron were full of wrath, and they made war on the men of Calydon. Many times they fought, but in every battle the strong arm of Meleagros and his stout heart won the victory for the men of his own city; and the Curêtes began to grow faint in spirit, so that they quailed before the

spear and sword of Meleagros. But presently
Meleagros was seen no more with his people, and
his voice was no longer heard cheering them on
to the battle. No more would he take lance in
hand or lift up his shield for the strife, but he
tarried in his own house by the side of the beautiful Cleopatra, whom Idas her father gave to him
to be his wife.

For the heart of his mother was filled with
grief and rage when she heard the story of the
deadly strife, and that Meleagros, her child, had
slain her brother. In heavy wrath and sorrow
she sat down upon the earth, and she cast the
dust from the ground into the air, and with wild
words called on Hades, the unseen king, and Persephone who shares his dark throne : ' Lord
of the lands beneath the earth, stretch forth
thy hand against Meleagros, my child. He has
quenched the love of a mother in my brother's
blood, and I will that he should die.' And even
as she prayed, the awful Erinnys which wanders
through the air, heard her words and sware to
accomplish the doom. But Meleagros was yet
more wrathful when he knew that his mother had
laid her curse upon him; and therefore he would
not go forth out of his chamber to the aid of his
people in the war.

So the Curêtes grew more and more mighty; and their warriors came up against the city of Calydon, and would no longer suffer the people to come without the walls. And everywhere there was faintness of heart and grief of spirit, for the enemy had wasted their fields and slain the bravest of the men, and little store remained to them of food. Day by day Œneus besought his son, and the great men of the city fell at the knees of Meleagros and prayed him to come out to their help, but he would not hearken. Still he tarried in his chamber with his wife Cleopatra by his side, and heeded not the hunger and the wailings of the people. Fiercer and fiercer waxed the roar of war; the loosened stones rolled from the tottering wall, and the battered gates were scarce able to keep out the enemy. Then Cleopatra fell at her husband's knee, and she took him by the hand and called him gently by his name, and said, 'O Meleagros, if thou wilt think of thy wrath, think also of the evils which war brings with it,— how, when a city is taken, the men are slain, and the mother with her child, the old and the young, are borne away into slavery. If the men of Pleurôn win the day, thy mother may repent her of the curse which she has laid upon thee; but thou wilt see thy children slain and me a slave.' Then Meleagros started from his couch and seized his spear and shield. He spake no word, but hastened to the walls; and soon the men of Calydon fell back before the spear which never missed its mark. Then he gathered the warriors of his city, and bade them open the gates, and went forth against the enemy. Long and dreadful was the battle, but at length the Curêtes turned and fled, and the danger passed away from the men of Calydon.

But the Mœræ still remembered the doom of the burning brand, and the unpitying Erinnys had not forgotten the curse of Althæa; and they moved the men of Calydon to withhold the prize of his good deeds from the chieftain Meleagros. 'He came not forth,' they said, 'save at the prayer of his wife. He hearkened not when we besought him; he heeded not our misery and tears: why should we give him that which he did not win from any love for us?' So his people were angry with Meleagros, and his spirit grew yet more bitter within him. Once again he lay within his own chamber, and his spear and shield hung idle on the wall; and it pleased him more to listen the whole day long to the soft words of Cleopatra, than to be doing brave and good deeds for the people of his land. Then the heart of his

mother Althæa was more and more turned away
from him, so that she said in bitterness of spirit,
'What good shall his life now do to me?' and
she brought forth the half-burnt brand from its
secret place, and cast it on the hearth. Suddenly
it burst into a flame, and suddenly the strength
of Meleagros began to fail as he lay in the arms
of Cleopatra. 'My life is wasting within me,' he
said; 'clasp me closer in thine arms; let others
lay a curse upon me, so only I die rejoicing in
thy love.' Weaker and weaker grew his failing
breath, but still he looked with his loving eyes on
the face of Cleopatra, and his spirit went forth
with a sigh of gladness, as the last spark of the
brand flickered out upon the hearth.

Then was there grief and sorrow in the house
of Œneus and through all the city of Calydon,
but they wept and mourned in vain. They thought
now of his good deeds, his wise counsels, and his
mighty arm; but in vain they bewailed the death
of their chieftain in the glory of his age. Yet
deeper and more bitter was the sorrow of Althæa,
for the love of a mother came back to her heart
when the Mœræ had accomplished the doom of
her child. And yet more bitterly sorrowed his
wife Cleopatra, and yearned for the love which had
been torn away from her. There was no more

joy within the halls of Œneus, for the Erinnys had done her task well. Soon Althæa followed her child to the unknown land, and Cleopatra went forth with joy to meet Meleagros in the dark kingdom of Hades and Persephonê.

PHAETHON.

IN the golden house which Hephæstos had wrought for him with his wondrous skill, Helios saw nothing fairer than his son Phaethon; and he said to his mother Clymenê, that no mortal child might be matched with him for beauty. And Phaethon heard the words, and his heart was filled with an evil pride. So he stood before the throne of Helios and said, 'O father who dwellest in the dazzling light, they say that I am thy child; but how shall I know it while I live in thy house without name and glory? Give me a token, that men may know me to be thy son.' Then Helios bade him speak, and sware to grant his prayer; and Phaethon said, 'I will guide thy chariot for one day through the high heaven; bid the Horæ make ready the horses for me, when Eôs spreads her quivering light in the sky.' But the heart of Helios was filled with fear, and he besought his son with many tears to call back his words. 'O Phaethon, bright child of Clymenê, for all thy beauty, thou art mortal.

still; and the horses of Helios obey no earthly master.' But Phaethon hearkened not to his words, and hastened away to the dwelling of the Horæ who guard the fiery horses. 'Make ready for me,' he said, 'the chariot of Helios, for this day I go through the high heaven in the stead of my father.'

The fair-haired Eôs spread her faint light in the pale sky, and Lampetiê was driving the cattle of Helios to their bright pastures [71], when the Horæ brought forth his horses and harnessed them to the fiery chariot. With eager hand Phaethon seized the reins, and the horses sped upon their way up the heights of the blue heaven, until the heart of Phaethon was full of fear and the reins quivered in his grasp. Wildly and more madly sped the steeds, till at last they hurried from the track which led to the Hesperian land. Down from their path they plunged and drew near to the broad plains of earth. Fiercer and fiercer flashed the scorching flames; the trees bowed down their withered heads; the green grass shrivelled on the hillsides; the rivers vanished from their slimy beds, and the black vapours rose with smoke and fire from the hidden depths of the mighty hills. Then in every land the sons of men lay dying on the scorched and gaping ground. They looked up to the yellow sky, but the clouds came not; they looked for the rivers and fountains, but no water glistened on their slimy beds; and young and old, all lay down in madness of heart to sleep the sleep of death.

So sped the horses of Helios on their fiery wanderings, and Zeus looked down from his Thessalian hill, and saw that all living things on the earth must die, unless Phaethon should be smitten down from his father's chariot. Then the mighty thunders woke in the hot sky, which mourned for the clouds that were dead; and the streams of lightning rushed forth upon Phaethon, and bore him from the blazing heaven far down beneath the waters of the green sea.

But his sisters wept sore for the death of the bright Phaethon, and the daughters of Hesperus built his tomb on the sea-shore, that all men might remember the name of the son of Helios and say, 'Phaethon fell from his father's chariot, but he lost not his glory, for his heart was set upon great things.'[22]

EPIMÈTHEUS AND PANDORA.

THERE was strife between Zeus and men; for Prometheus stood forth on their side and taught them how they might withstand the new god who sat on the throne of Cronos: and he said, 'O men, Zeus is greedy of riches and honour; and your flocks and herds will be wasted with burnt offerings, if ye offer up to Zeus the whole victim. Come and let us make a covenant with him, that there may be a fair portion for him and for men.' So Prometheus chose out a large ox, and slew him, and divided the body. Under the skin he placed the entrails and the flesh, and under the fat he placed the bones. Then he said, 'Choose thy portion, O Zeus; and let that on which thou layest thine hands be thy share for ever.' So Zeus stretched forth his hand in haste and placed it upon the fat; and fierce was his wrath when he found only the bare bones underneath it. Wherefore men offer up to the undying gods only the bones and fat of the victims that are slain.

Then in his anger Zeus sought how he might avenge himself on the race of men; and he took away from them the gift of fire [22], so that they were vexed by cold and darkness and hunger, until Prometheus brought them down fire which he had stolen from heaven. Then was the rage of Zeus still more cruel, and he smote Prometheus with his thunderbolts; and at his bidding Hermes bare him to the crags of Caucasus, and bound him with iron chains to the hard rock, where the vulture gnawed his heart with its beak.

But the wrath of Zeus was not appeased, and he sought how he might yet more vex the race of men; and he remembered how the Titan Prometheus warned them to accept no gift from the gods, and how he left his brother Epimêtheus to guard them against the wiles of the son of Cronos. And he said within himself, 'The race of men knows neither sickness or pain, strife or war, theft or falsehood; for all these evil things are sealed up in the great cask which is guarded by Epimêtheus. I will let loose these evils, and the whole earth shall be filled with woe and misery.'

So he called Hephæstos, the lord of fire; and he said, 'Make ready a gift which all the undying gods shall give to the race of man. Take earth, and fashion it into the shape of woman. Very fair let it be to look upon, but give her an evil nature, that the race of men may suffer for all the deeds that they have done to me.' Then Hephæstos took the clay and moulded from it the image of a fair woman, and Athene clothed her in a beautiful robe, and placed a crown upon her head, from which a veil fell over her snowy shoulders. And Hermes, the messenger of Zeus, gave her the power of words, and a greedy mind, to cheat and deceive the race of men. Then Hephæstos brought her before the assembly of the gods, and they marvelled at the greatness of her beauty; and Zeus took her by the hand and gave her to Epimêtheus, and said, 'Ye toil hard, O race of men: behold one who shall soothe and cheer you when the hours of toil are ended. The undying gods have taken pity on you, because ye have none to comfort you; and woman is their gift to men, therefore is her name called Pandora.'[24]

Then Epimêtheus forgot the warning of his brother, and the race of men did obeisance to Zeus, and received Pandora at his hands; for the greatness of her beauty enslaved the hearts of all who looked upon her. But they rejoiced not long in the gift of the gods; for Pandora saw a great k on the threshold of the house of Epimêtheus, and she lifted the lid; and from it came strife and war, plague and sickness, theft and violence, grief and sorrow. Then in her terror she set down the lid again upon the cask, and Hope was shut up within it, so that she could not comfort the race of men for the grievous evil which Pandora had brought upon them.

IÓ AND PROMETHEUS.

IN the halls of Inachos, king of Argos, Zeus beheld and loved the fair maiden Iô; but when Hêrê the queen knew it, she was very wroth and sought to slay her. Then Zeus changed the maiden into a heifer, to save her from the anger of Hêrê; but presently Hêrê learned that the heifer was the maiden whom she hated, and she went to Zeus and said, 'Give me that which I shall desire;' and Zeus answered, 'Say on.' Then Hêrê said, 'Give me the beautiful heifer which I see feeding in the pastures of King Inachos.' So Zeus granted her prayer, for he liked not to confess what he had done to Iô to save her from the wrath of Hêrê; and Hêrê took the heifer and bade Argus with the hundred eyes watch over it by night and by day.

Long time Zeus sought how he might deliver the maiden from the vengeance of Hêrê; but he strove in vain, for Argus never slept, and his hundred eyes saw everything around him, and none could approach without being seen and slain.

At the last Zeus sent Hermes, the bright messenger
of the gods, who stole gently towards Argus,
playing soft music on his lute. Soothingly the
sweet sounds fell upon his ear, and a deep sleep
began to weigh down his eyelids, until Argus with
the hundred eyes lay powerless before Hermes.
Then Hermes drew his sharp sword, and with a
single stroke he smote off his head; wherefore
men call him the slayer of Argus with the hundred
eyes. But the wrath of Hêrê was fiercer than ever,
when she learned that her watchman was slain;
and she sware that the heifer should have no rest,
but wander in terror and pain from land to land.
So she sent a gadfly to goad the heifer with its
fiery sting over hill and valley, across sea and
river, to torment her if she lay down to rest, and
madden her with pain when she sought to sleep.
In grief and madness she fled from the pastures
of Inachos, past the city of Erectheus into the
land of Cadmus the Theban. On and on still she
went, resting not by night or day, through the
Dorian and Thessalian plains, until at last she
came to the wild Thracian land. Her feet bled
on the sharp stones; her body was torn by the
thorns and brambles, and tortured by the stings
of the fearful gadfly. Still she fled on and on,
while the tears streamed often down her cheeks,

and her moaning showed the greatness of her agony. 'O Zeus,' she said, 'dost thou not see me in my misery? Thou didst tell me once of thy love; and dost thou suffer me now to be driven thus wildly from land to land, without hope of comfort or rest? Slay me at once, I pray thee, or suffer me to sink into the deep sea, that so I may put off the sore burden of my woe.'

But Iô knew not that, while she spake, one heard her who had suffered even harder things from Zeus. Far above her head, towards the desolate crags of Caucasus, the wild eagle soared shrieking in the sky; and the vulture hovered near, as though waiting close to some dying man till death should leave him for its prey. Dark snow-clouds brooded heavily on the mountain, the icy wind crept lazily through the frozen air; and Iô thought that the hour of her death was come. Then, as she raised her head, she saw far off a giant form, which seemed fastened by nails to the naked rock; and a low groan reached her ear, as of one in mortal pain, and she heard a voice which said, 'Whence comest thou, daughter of Inachos, into this savage wilderness? Hath the love of Zeus driven thee thus to the icy corners of the earth?' Then Iô gazed at him in wonder and awe, and said, 'How dost thou know my

name and my sorrows? and what is thine own
wrong? Tell me (if it is given to thee to know)
what awaits thee and me in the time to come; for
sure I am that thou art no mortal man. Thy giant
form is as the form of gods or heroes, who come
down sometimes to mingle with the sons of men;
and great must be the wrath of Zeus, that thou
shouldst be thus tormented here.' Then he said,
'O maiden, thou seest the Titan Prometheus
who brought down fire for the children of men,
and taught them how to build themselves houses
and till the earth, and how to win for themselves
food and clothing.[25] I gave them wise thoughts
and good laws and prudent counsel, and raised
them from the life of beasts to a life which was
fit for speaking men. But the son of Cronos
was afraid at my doings, lest, with the aid of men,
I might hurl him from his place and set up new
gods upon his throne. So he forgot all my good
deeds in time past, how I had aided him when
the earth-born giants sought to destroy his power
and heaped rock on rock and crag on crag to
smite him on his throne; and he caught me by
craft, telling me in smooth words how that he
was my friend, and that my honour should not
fail in the halls of Olympus. So he took me
unawares and bound me with iron chains, and

bade Hephæstos take and fasten me to this mountain side, where the frost and wind and heat scorch and torment me by day and night, and the vulture gnaws my heart with its merciless beak. But my spirit is not wholly cast down; for I know that I have done good to the sons of men, and that they honour the Titan Prometheus, who has saved them from cold and hunger and sickness. And well I know, also, that the reign of Zeus shall one day come to an end, and that another shall sit at length upon his throne, even as now he sits on the throne of his father Cronos. Hither come, also, those who seek to comfort me; and thou seest before thee the daughters of Okeanos, who have but now arrived to talk with me from the green halls of their father. Listen then to me, O daugher of Inachos, and I will tell thee what shall befall thee in time to come. Hence, from the ice-bound chain of Caucasus, thou shalt roam into the Scythian land and the regions of the Chalybes. Thence thou shalt come to the dwelling-place of the Amâzons on the banks of the river Thermôdon; these shall guide thee on thy way, until at length thou shalt come to a strait, which thou wilt cross, and which shall tell by its name for ever where the heifer passed from Europe into Asia. But the end of thy wanderings is not yet.'

Then Iô could no longer repress her grief, and her tears burst forth afresh; and Prometheus said, 'O daughter of Inachos, if thou sorrowest thus at what I have told thee, how wilt thou bear to hear what beyond these things there remains for thee to do?' But Iô said, 'Of what use is it, O Titan, to tell me of these woful wanderings? Better were it now to die and be at rest from all this misery and sorrow.' 'Nay, not so, O maiden of Argos,' said Prometheus, 'for if thou livest, the days will come when Zeus shall be cast down from his throne; and the end of his reign shall also be the end of my sufferings. For when thou hast passed by the Thracian Bosporus into the land of Asia, thou wilt wander on through many regions, where the Gorgons dwell and the Arimaspi and Ethiopians, until at last thou shalt come to the three-cornered land where the mighty Nile goes out by its many arms into the sea. There shall be thy resting-place, and there shall Epaphos, thy son, be born, from whom, in times yet far away, shall spring the great Heracles, who shall break my chain and set me free from my long torments. And if in this thou doubtest my words, I can tell thee of every land through which thou hast passed on thy journey hither; but it is enough if I tell thee how the speaking oaks of Dodona hailed thee as one day to be the wife of Zeus and the mother of the mighty Epaphos. Hasten, then, on thy way, O daughter of Inachos. Long years of pain and sorrow await thee still; but my griefs shall endure for many generations. It avails not now to weep; but this comfort thou hast, that thy lot is happier than mine; and for both of us remains the surety that the right shall at last conquer, and the power of Zeus shall be brought low, even as the power of Cronos whom he hurled from his ancient throne. Depart hence quickly, for I see Hermes the messenger drawing nigh, and perchance he comes with fresh torments for thee and me.'

So Iô went on her weary road, and Hermes drew nigh to Prometheus, and bade him once again yield himself to the will of the mighty Zeus. But Prometheus laughed him to scorn; and as Hermes turned to go away, the icy wind came shrieking through the air, and the dark cloud sank lower and lower down the hillside, until it covered the rock on which the body of the Titan was nailed; and the great mountain heaved with the earthquake, and the blazing thunderbolts darted fearfully through the sky. Brighter and brighter flashed the lightning, and louder pealed the thunder in the ears of Prometheus;

but he quailed not for all the fiery majesty of Zeus; and still, as the storm grew fiercer and the curls of fire were wreathed around his form, his voice was heard amid the din and roar, and it spake of the day when the good shall triumph and unjust power shall be crushed and destroyed for ever.

BRIAREÓS.

THERE was strife in the halls of Olympus, for Zeus had conquered the ancient gods, and sat on the throne of his father Cronos. In his hand he held the thunderbolts; the lightning slumbered at his feet; and around him all the gods trembled for the greatness of his power. For he laid hard tasks on all, and spake hard words; and he thought to rule harshly over the gods who dwell on the earth and in the broad sea. All the day long Hermes toiled on weary errands to do his will; for Zeus sought to crush all alike, and remembered not the time when he too was weak and powerless.

Then were there secret whisperings, as the gods of earth and sea took counsel together; and Poseidon, the lord of the dark waters, spake in fierce anger and said, 'Hearken to me, O Hêrê and Athene, and let us rise up against Zeus, and teach him that he has not power over all. See ye how he bears himself in his new majesty,— how he thinks not of the aid which we gave him in the war with his father Cronos,—how he has smitten down even the mightiest of his friends. For Prometheus, who gave fire to mortal men and saved them from biting cold and gnawing hunger, lies chained on the crags of Caucasus; and if he shrink not to bind the Titan, see that he smite not thee also in his wrath, O lady Hêrê.' And Athene said, 'The wisdom of Zeus is departed from him, and all his deeds are done now in craft and falsehood; let us bind him fast, lest all the heaven and earth be filled with strife and war.' So they vowed a vow that they would no more bear the tyranny of Zeus; and Hephæstos forged strong chains at their bidding to cast around him when sleep lay heavy on his eyelids.

But Thetis heard the words of Poseidon and Athene, as she sat beneath the waters in her coral cave; and she rose up like a white mist from the sea, and knelt before the throne of Zeus. Then she clasped her arms round his knees and said, ' O Zeus, the gods tremble at thy might, but they love not thy hard words; and they say that thy wisdom hath departed from thee, and that thou doest all things in craft and falsehood. Hearken to me, O Zeus; for Hephæstos hath forged the chain, and the lady Hêrê, and Poseidon the lord of the sea, and the pure Athene have vowed a vow to bind thee fast when sleep lies heavy on thine eyes. Let me therefore go, that I may bring Briareôs to aid thee with his hundred hands; and when he sits by thy side, then shalt thou need no more to fear the wrath of Hêrê and Poseidon. And when the peril is past, then, O Zeus, remember that thou must rule gently and justly, for that power shall not stand which fights with truth and love; and forget not those who aid thee, or reward them as thou hast rewarded Prometheus on the crags of Caucasus; for it may be that, in time to come, I may ask a boon from thee for Achilleus my child, who dwells now in the house of his father Peleus; and when that hour shall come, then call to mind how in time past I saved thee from the chains of Hephæstos.'

Then Zeus spake gently, and said, 'Hasten, O Thetis, and bring hither the mighty Briareôs that he may guard me with his hundred hands; and fear not for the words that thou hast spoken, for Zeus will not cast aside good counsel, and the gods shall hate me no more for hard and unkindly words.'

So, from the depths of the inmost earth, Thetis summoned Briareôs to the aid of Zeus; and presently his giant form was seen in the hall of Olympus, and the gods trembled as he sat down by the side of Zeus, exulting in the greatness of his strength. And Zeus spake and said, 'Hearken to me, O lady Hêrê, and Poseidon, and Athene. I know your counsels, and how ye purposed to bind me for my evil deeds; but fear not. Only do my bidding in time to come, and ye shall no more have cause to say that Zeus is a hard and cruel master.' [26]

SEMELÊ.

THROUGH all the Bœotian land, Semelê, the daughter of King Cadmus, was known for her great beauty; and when Zeus looked on her in her father's house at Thebes, he loved the maiden, and it wakened the wrath of Hêrê, so that she sought how she might slay her. And when she knew that Zeus went many times down from Olympus to see the daughter of Cadmus, she bade Beroê, her nurse, go to Semelê and cheat her into her ruin. So Beroê went and spake crafty words to Semelê, and told her of the glories of Olympus. 'There Zeus dwells,' she said, 'high up above the dark clouds; and the thunder roars and the lightning flashes about his throne. There his fiery horses bear him in terrible majesty when he goes to visit Hêrê the queen, and the sun is blotted out from the sky in the thick darkness which he spreads around him.' Then Beroê hastened away, for her work was done; and Semelê pondered on the words which she had heard, and when Zeus came again, she said to him, 'Why comest thou to me always so calmly and gently? I love to see thee kind and tender to me, but I seek also to behold thy majesty. Come to me once as thou art when thou goest to see Hêrê the queen.' Then Zeus said, 'Ah, Semelê, thou knowest not what thou wouldst have. Hêrê, the queen, is of the race of the bright gods, and immortal blood flows in her veins; but thou art the child of mortal man, and thine eyes will fail before the blinding glare of my lightnings, and thy form be scorched by the searing flame.' But Semelê answered gaily, 'O Zeus, it cannot be so fearful as thou sayest; else even the race of the bright gods would quail before thy splendour. But thou hast promised long ago to grant me whatsoever I shall ask of thee, and I would that thou shouldst come to me in all thy great glory.' So Zeus promised to come as she wished, although he knew that then Semelê must die. Not long after, as she sat alone, there came a deep stillness over the air. She heard no sound, but a great horror fell on her and she felt as if she were taken away far from all help of men; and suddenly from the dead stillness burst the angry lightnings, and the blazing flame scorched up her body, as Zeus drew near to meet her. So, amidst the blaze of the lightning and the crashing of the thunderbolts, her child Dionysos was born.

Long time Semelê wandered in the land of shadows beneath the earth, until Dionysos had grown up into manhood and become the god of the feast and winecup. Then he went down to the kingdom of Hades, and led his mother away from her dark home[37], and Zeus and all the gods welcomed her by the name of Thyônê as she entered the halls of Olympus.

PENTHEUS.

FOR many years Dionysos wandered far away from the land of his birth; and wherever he went, he taught the people of the country to worship him as a god, and showed them strange rites. Far away he roamed, to the regions where the Ganges rolls his mighty stream into the Indian sea, and where the Nile brings every year rich gifts from the southern mountains. And in all the lands to which he came, he made the women gather round him and honour him with wild cries and screams and marvellous customs such as they had never known before. As he went onwards, the face of the land was changed. The women grouped themselves in companies far away from the sight of man, and, high up on the barren hills or down in the narrow valleys, with wild movements and fierce shoutings, paid honour to Dionysos, the lord of the winecup and the feast. At length, through the Thracian highlands and the soft plains of Thessaly, Dionysos came back to Thebes, where he had been born amid the roar of the thunder and the blaze of the fiery lightning. And Cadmus the king, who had built the city, was now old and weak, and he had made Pentheus, the child of his daughter Agavê, king in his stead. So Pentheus sought to rule the people well, as his father Cadmus had done, and to train them in the old laws, that they might be quiet in the days of peace and orderly and brave in war. And so it was that when Dionysos came near to Thebes, and commanded all the people to receive the new rites which he sought to teach them, it grieved Pentheus at the heart; and when he saw how the women seemed smitten with madness, and that they wandered away in groups to desert places, where they lurked for many days and nights far from the sight of man, he mourned for the evils which his kinsman Dionysos was bringing upon the land. So King Pentheus made a law that none should follow these new customs, and that the women should stay quietly, doing their own work in their homes. But when they heard this, they were all full of fury, for Dionysos had deceived them by his treacherous words, and even Cadmus himself, in his weakness and his old age, had been led astray by them. In crowds they thronged around the house of Pentheus and raised loud shouts in honour of Dionysos, and

besought him to follow the new way; but he
would not hearken to them. Thus it was for
many days; and when all the city was shaken by
the madness of the new worship, Pentheus thought
that he would see with his own eyes the strange
rites by which the women in their lurking-places
did honour to Dionysos. So he went secretly to
some hidden dells whither he knew that the
women had gone; but Dionysos saw him and
laid his hands upon him, and straightway the
mind of King Pentheus himself was darkened,
and the madness of the worshippers was upon him
also. Then in his folly he climbed a tall pine
tree, to see what the women did in their revelry;
but on a sudden one of them saw him, and they
shrieked wildly and rooted up the tree in their
fury. Then with one accord they seized Pentheus
and tore him in pieces; and his own mother
Agavê was among the first to lay hands on her
son. So Dionysos the wine god triumphed; and
this was the way in which the new worship was
set up in the Hellenic land.[26]

ARETHUSA.[29]

ON the heights of Mænalos the hunter Alpheios saw the maiden Arethusa as she wandered joyously with her companions over the green swelling downs where the heather spread out its pink blossoms to the sky. Onward she came, the fairest of all the band, until she drew nigh to the spot where Alpheios stood marvelling at the brightness of her beauty. Then, as she followed the winding path on the hillside, she saw his eye resting upon her, and her heart was filled with fear, for his dark face was flushed by the toil of the long chase, and his torn raiment waved wildly in the breeze. And yet more was she afraid when she heard the sound of his rough voice, as he prayed her to tarry by his side. She lingered not to listen to his words, but with light foot she sped over hill and dale and along the bank of the river where it leaps down the mountain cliffs and winds along the narrow valleys.

Then Alpheios vowed a vow that the maiden should not escape him. 'I will follow thee,' he said, 'over hill and dale, I will seek thee through rivers and seas; and where thou shalt rest, there will I rest also.' Onward they sped, across the dark heights of Erymanthos and over the broad plains of Pisa, till the waters of the western sea lay spread out before them, dancing in the light of the midday sun. Then with arms outstretched, and with wearied limbs, Arethusa cried aloud and said, 'O daughters of the gentle Okeanos, I have played with you on the white shore in the days of mirth and gladness; and now I come to your green depths. Save me from the hand of the wild huntsman.' So she plunged beneath the waves of the laughing sea, and the daughters of Okeanos bare her gently downwards till she came to the coral caves where they sat listening to the sweet song of the waters. But there they suffered her not to rest, for they said, 'Yet further must thou flee, O Arethusa; for Alpheios comes behind thee.' Then in their arms they bare her gently beneath the depths of the sea, till they laid her down at last on the Ortygian shore of the Thrinakian land, as the sun was sinking down in the sky. Dimly she saw spread before her the blue hills, and she felt the soft breath of the summer breeze, as her eyes closed for very weariness. Then suddenly she heard the harsh voice which scared her on the heights of Mænalos; and she tarried not to listen to his prayer. 'O Arethusa, flee not away,' said the huntsman Alpheios; 'I mean not to harm thee; let me rest in thy love, and let me die for the beauty of thy fair face.' But the maiden fled with a wild cry along the winding shore, and the light step of her foot left no print on the glistening sand. 'Not thus shalt thou escape from my arms,' said the huntsman Alpheios; and he stretched forth his hand to seize the maiden, as she drew nigh to a fountain whose waters flashed clear and bright in the light of the sinking sun. Then once again Arethusa called aloud on the daughters of Okeanos, and she said, 'O friends, once more I come to your coral caves, for on earth there is for me no resting-place.' So the waters closed over the maiden, and the image of heaven came down again on the bright fountain. Then a flush of anger passed over the face of Alpheios, as he said, 'On earth thou hast scorned my love, O maiden; but my form shall be fairer in thy sight when I rest beside thee beneath the laughing waters.' So over the huntsman Alpheios flowed the Ortygian stream; and the love of Arethusa was given to him in the coral caves where they dwell with the daughters of Okeanos.

TYRÔ.

ON the banks of the fairest stream in all the land of Thessaly, the golden-haired Enipeus wooed the maiden Tyrô: with her he wandered in gladness of heart, following the path of the winding river, and talking with her of his love. And Tyrô listened to his tender words, as day by day she stole away from the house of her father Salmoneus, to spend the livelong day on the banks of his beautiful stream.

But Salmoneus was full of rage when he knew that Tyrô loved Enipeus, and how she had become the mother of two fair babes. There was none to plead for Tyrô and her helpless children; for her mother Alkidikê was dead, and Salmoneus had taken the iron-hearted Sidêro [30] to be his wife. So he followed her evil counsels, and he said to Tyrô, 'Thy children must die, and thou must wed Cretheus, the son of the mighty Æolus.'

Then Tyrô hastened in bitter sorrow to the banks of the stream, and her babes slept in her arms; and she stretched out her hands with a loud cry for aid, but Enipeus heard her not, for he lay in his green dwelling far down beneath the happy waters. So she placed the babes amidst the thick rushes which grew along the banks, and she said, 'O Enipeus, my father says that I may no more see thy face; but to thee I give our children : guard them from the anger of Salmoneus, and it may be that in time to come they will avenge my wrongs.'

There, nestled amid the tall reeds, the children slept, till a herdsman saw them as he followed his cattle along the shore. And Tyrô went back in anguish of heart to the house of Salmoneus, but she would not have the love of Cretheus or listen to his words. Then Sidêro whispered again her evil counsels into the ear of Salmoneus, and he shut up Tyrô, so that she might not see the light of the sun or hear the voice of man. He cut off the golden locks that clustered on her fair cheeks; he clothed her in rough raiment, and bound her in fetters which gave her no rest by night or by day. So in her misery she pined away, and her body was wasted by hunger and thirst, because she would not become the wife of Cretheus. Then more and more she thought of the days when she listened to the words of Enipeus as she wandered with him by the side of the

sounding waters; and she said within herself,
'He heard me not when I called to him for help,
but I gave him my children, and it may be that
he has saved them from death; and if ever they
see my face again, they shall know that I never
loved any save Enipeus, who dwells beneath
the stream.'

So the years passed on, and Pelius and Neleus
dwelt with the herdsman, and they grew up strong
in body and brave of soul. But Enipeus had not
forgotten the wrongs of Tyrô, and he put it into
the heart of her children to punish Sidêro for her
evil counsels. So Sidêro died, and they brought
out their mother from her dreary dungeon, and
led her to the banks of the stream where she had
heard the words of Enipeus in the former days.
But her eyes were dim with long weeping, and
the words of her children sounded strangely in her
ears; and she said, 'O my children, let me sink
to sleep while I hear your voices, which sound to
me like the voice of Enipeus.' So she fell asleep
and died, and they laid her body in the ground
by the river's bank, where the waters of Enipeus
made their soft music near her grave.[31]

POSEIDON AND ATHENE.[52]

NEAR the banks of the stream Kephisos, Erectheus had built a city in a rocky and thin-soiled land. He was the father of a free and brave people; and though his city was small and humble, yet Zeus by his wisdom foresaw that one day it would become the noblest of all cities throughout the wide earth. And there was a strife between Poseidon the lord of the sea, and Athene the virgin child of Zeus, to see by whose name the city of Erectheus should be called. So Zeus appointed a day in the which he would judge between them in presence of the great gods who dwell on high Olympus.

When the day was come, the gods sat each on his golden throne, on the banks of the stream Kephisos. High above all was the throne of Zeus, the great father of gods and men, and by his side sat Hêrê the queen. This day even the sons of men might gaze upon them, for Zeus had laid aside his lightnings, and all the

gods had come down in peace to listen to his judgment between Poseidon and Athene. There sat Phœbus Apollo with his golden harp in his hand. His face glistened for the brightness of his beauty; but there was no anger in his gleaming eye, and idle by his side lay the unerring spear with which he smites all who deal falsely and speak lies.[33] There beside him sat Artemis, his sister, whose days were spent in chasing the beasts of the earth, and in sporting with the nymphs on the reedy banks of Eurôtas. There by the side of Zeus sat Hermes, ever bright and youthful, the spokesman of the gods, with staff in hand to do the will of the great father. There sat Hephæstos the lord of fire, and Hestia who guards the hearth. There, too, was Ares, who delights in war; and Dionysos, who loves the banquet and the winecup; and Aphroditê, who rose from the sea-foam to fill the earth with laughter and woe.

Before them all stood the great rivals, awaiting the judgment of Zeus. High in her left hand, Athene held the invincible spear; and on her ægis, hidden from mortal sight, was the face on which no man may gaze and live. Close beside her, proud in the greatness of his power, Poseidon waited the issue of the contest. In his right hand gleamed the trident with which he shakes the earth and cleaves the waters of the sea.

Then from his golden seat rose the spokesman Hermes; and his clear voice sounded over all the great council. 'Listen,' he said, 'to the will of Zeus, who judges now between Poseidon and Athene. The city of Erectheus shall bear the name of that god who shall bring forth out of the earth the best gift for the sons of men. If Poseidon do this, the city shall be called Poseidonia; but if Athene brings the higher gift, it shall be called Athens.'

Then King Poseidon rose up in the greatness of his majesty, and with his trident he smote the earth where he stood. Straightway the hill was shaken to its depths, and the earth clave asunder, and forth from the chasm leaped a horse, such as never shall be seen again for strength and beauty. His body shone white all over as the driven snow; his mane streamed proudly in the wind as he stamped on the ground and scoured in very wantonness over hill and valley. 'Behold my gift,' said Poseidon, 'and call the city after my name. Who shall give aught better than the horse to the sons of men?'

But Athene looked steadfastly at the gods with her keen grey eye; and she stooped slowly down

to the ground and planted in it a little seed which
she held in her right hand. She spake no word,
but still gazed calmly on that great council. Presently they saw springing from the earth a little
germ, which grew up and threw out its boughs and
leaves. Higher and higher it rose, with all its
thick green foliage, and put forth fruit on its
clustering branches. 'My gift is better, O Zeus,'
she said, 'than that of King Poseidon. The
horse which he has given shall bring war and
strife and anguish to the children of men; my
olive-tree is the sign of peace and plenty, of health
and strength, and the pledge of happiness and
freedom. Shall not then the city of Erectheus be
called after my name?'[34]

Then with one accord rose the voices of the
gods in the air, as they cried out, 'The gift of
Athene is the best which may be given to the
sons of men; it is the token that the city of
Erectheus shall be greater in peace than in war,
and nobler in its freedom than its power. Let
the city be called by the name of Athena.'

Then Zeus, the mighty son of Cronos, bowed his
head in sign of judgment that the city should be
called Athens; from his head the immortal locks
streamed down [35], and the earth trembled beneath
his feet, as he rose from his golden throne to

return to the halls of Olympus. But still Athene stood gazing over the land which was now her own; and she stretched out her spear towards the city of Erectheus, and said, 'I have won the victory, and here shall be my home. Here shall my children grow up in happiness and freedom; and hither shall the sons of men come to learn of law and order. Here shall they see what great things may be done by mortal hands when aided by the gods who dwell on Olympus; and when the torch of freedom has gone out at Athens, its light shall be handed on to other lands, and men shall learn that my gift is still the best, and they shall say that reverence for law and the freedom of thought and deed has come to them from the city of Erectheus which bears the name of Athene.'

ARIADNÊ.

THE soft western breeze was bearing a ship from the Athenian land to the fair haven of Gnossos; and the waters played merrily round the ship as it sped along the paths of the sea. But on board there were mournful hearts and weeping eyes, for the youths and maidens which that ship was bearing to Crete were to be the prey of the savage Minotauros. As they came near the harbour gates, they saw the people of King Minos crowded on the shore, and they wept aloud because they should no more look on the earth and on the sun as he journeyed through the heaven.

In that throng stood Ariadnê the daughter of the king, and as she gazed on the youths and maidens who came out of the tribute ship, there passed before her one taller and fairer than all; and she saw that his eye alone was bright and his step firm, as he moved from the shore to go to the house of Minos. Presently they all stood before the king, and he saw that one alone gazed steadfastly upon him, while the eyes of all the rest were made dim with many tears. Then he said, 'What is thy name, O youth?' and the young man answered, 'I am Theseus, the son of King Ægeus, and I have come as one of the tribute children; but I part not with my life till I have battled for it with all my strength. Wherefore send me first, I pray thee, that I may fight with Minotauros; for if I be the conqueror, then shall all these go back with me in peace to our own land.' But Minos said, 'Thou shalt indeed go first to meet Minotauros; but think not to conquer him in the fight, for the flame from his mouth will scorch thee, and no mortal man may withstand his strength.' And Theseus answered, 'It is for man to do what best he may; the gods know for whom remains the victory.'

But the gentle heart of Ariadnê was moved with love and pity as she looked on his fair face and his bright and fearless eye; and she said within herself, 'I cannot kill the Minotauros or rob him of his strength, but I will guide Theseus so that he may reach the monster while sleep lies heavy upon him.'

On the next day Theseus, the Athenian, was to meet the dreadful Minotauros who dwelt in the labyrinth of Gnossos. Far within its thousand twisted alleys was his den, where he waited for his prey, as they were brought each along the winding paths. But Ariadnê talked in secret with Theseus in the still evening time, and she gave him a clue of thread, so that he might know how to come back out of the mazes of the labyrinth after he had slain the Minotauros; and when the moon looked down from heaven, she led him to a hidden gate, and bade him go forth boldly, for he should come to the monster's den while sleep lay heavy on his eyes. So when the morning came, the Minotauros lay lifeless on the ground; and there was joy and gladness in the great city of Gnossos, and Minos himself rejoiced that the youths and maidens might go back with Theseus in peace to Athens.

So once again they went into the ship, and the breeze blew softly to carry them to the homes which they had not thought to see again. But Theseus talked with Ariadnê in the house of Minos, and the maiden wept as though some great grief lay heavy upon her; and Theseus twined his arm gently round her and said, 'O fairest of maidens, thy aid hath saved me from death; but I care not now to live if I may not be with thee. Come with me, and I will lead thee to the happier land, where my father Ægeus is king. Come with me, that my people may see and love the maiden who rescued the tribute children from the savage Minotauros.'

Then Ariadnê went with him joyfully, for her own love made her think that Theseus loved her not less dearly. So she wept not as she saw the towers of Gnossos growing fainter and fainter while the ship sped over the dancing waters; and she thought only of the happy days which she should spend in the bright Athens where Theseus should one day be king. Gaily the ship sped upon her way, and there was laughter and mirth among the youths and maidens who were going back to their home. And Theseus sat by the side of Ariadnê, speaking the words of a deeper love than in truth he felt, and fancying that he loved the maiden even as the maiden loved him. But while yet he gazed on the beautiful Ariadnê, the image of Aiglê came back to his mind, and the old love was wakened again in his heart. Onward sailed the ship, cleaving its way through the foaming waters, by the islands of Thera and Amorgos, till the high cliffs of Naxos broke upon their sight.

The sun was sinking down into the sea when they came to its winding shores, and the seamen moored the ship to the land, and came forth to rest until the morning. There they feasted gaily on the beach, and Theseus talked with Ariadnê until the moon was high up in the sky. So they slept through the still hours of night; but when the sun was risen, Ariadnê was alone upon the sea-shore. In doubt and fear, she roamed along the beach, but she saw no one; and there was no ship sailing on the blue sea. In many a bay and nook she sought him, and she cried in bitter sorrow, 'Ah, Theseus, Theseus, hast thou forsaken me?' Her feet were wounded by the sharp flints, her limbs were faint from very weariness, and her eyes were dim with tears. Above her rose the high cliffs like a wall, before her was spread the bright and laughing sea; and her heart sank within her, for she felt that she must die. 'Ah, Theseus,' she cried, 'have I done thee wrong? I pitied thee in the time of thy sorrow and saved thee from thy doom; and then I listened to thy fair words, and trusted them as a maiden trusts when love is first awakened within her. Yet hast thou dealt me a hard requital. Thou art gone to happy Athens, and it may be thou thinkest already of some bright maiden who there has crossed thy path; and thou hast left me here to die for weariness and hunger. So would not I requite thee for a deed of love and pity.'

Wearied and sad of heart, she sank down on the rock; and her long hair streamed over her fair shoulders. Her hands were clasped around her knees, and the hot tears ran down her cheek; and she knew not that there stood before her one fairer and brighter than the sons of men, until she heard a voice which said, 'Listen to me, O daughter of Minos. I am Dionysos, the lord of the feast and revel. I wander with light heart and the sweet sounds of laughter and song over land and sea; I saw thee aid Theseus when he went into the labyrinth to slay the Minotauros. I heard his fair words when he prayed thee to leave thy home and go with him to Athens. I saw him this morning, while yet the stars twinkled in the sky, arouse his men and sail away in his ship to the land of Ægeus; but I sought not to stay him, for, Ariadnê, thou must dwell with me. Thy love and beauty is a gift too great for Theseus; but thou shalt be the bride of Dionysos. Thy days shall be passed amidst feasts and banquets; and when thy life is ended here, thou shalt go with me to the homes of the undying gods, and men shall see the crown of Ariadnê in the heavens when the stars look forth at night from the dark sky. Nay, weep not, Ariadnê; thy love for Theseus hath been but the love of a day, and I have loved thee long before the black-sailed ship brought him from poor and rugged Athens.'

Then Ariadnê wept no more, and in the arms of Dionysos she forgot the false and cruel Theseus; so that among the matrons who thronged round the joyous wine god, the fairest and the most joyous was Ariadnê the daughter of Minos.

NARCISSUS.

ON the banks of Kephisos, Echo saw and loved the beautiful Narcissus; but the youth cared not for the maiden of the hills, and his heart was cold to the words of her love, for he mourned for his sister [37] whom Hermes had taken away beyond the Stygian river. Day by day he sat alone by the stream side, sorrowing for the bright maiden whose life was bound up with his own, because they had seen the light of the sun in the selfsame day; and thither came Echo and sat down by his side, and sought in vain to win his love. 'Look on me and see,' she said; 'I am fairer than the sister for whom thou dost mourn.' But Narcissus answered her not, for he knew that the maiden would ever have something to say against his words. So he sat silent and looked down into the stream, for there he saw his own face in the clear water, and it was to him as the face of his sister for whom he pined away in sorrow; and his grief became less bitter as he seemed to see again her soft blue eye, and almost to hear the words which came from her lips. But the grief of Narcissus was too deep for tears, and it dried up slowly the fountain of his life. In vain the words of Echo fell upon his ears, as she prayed him to hearken to her prayer; 'Ah, Narcissus, thou mournest for one who cannot heed thy sorrow, and thou carest not for her who longs to see thy face and hear thy voice for ever.' But Narcissus saw still in the waters of Kephisos the face of his twin sister, and still gazing at it he fell asleep and died. Then the voice of Echo was heard no more, for she sat in silence by his grave; and a beautiful flower came up close to it. Its white blossoms drooped over the bank of Kephisos where Narcissus had sat and looked down into its clear water; and the people of the land called the plant after his name.

MEDEIA.

FAR away in the Colchian land, where her father Æetes was king, the wise maiden Medeia saw and loved Jason, who had come in the ship Argo to search for the golden fleece. To her Zeus had given a wise and cunning heart, and she had power over the hidden things of the earth, and nothing in the broad sea could withstand her might. She had spells to tame the monsters which vex the children of men, and to bring back youth to the wrinkled face and the tottering limbs of the old. But the spells of Eros were mightier still, and the wise maiden forgot her cunning as she looked on the fair countenance of Jason; and she said within herself that she would make him conqueror in his struggle for the golden fleece, and go with him to be his wife in the far-off western land. So King Æetes brought up in vain the fire-breathing bulls that they might scorch Jason as he ploughed the land with the dragon's teeth; and in vain from these teeth sprang up the harvest of armed men ready for strife and bloodshed. For Medeia had anointed the body of Jason with ointment, so that the fiery breath of the bulls hurt him not; and by her bidding he cast a stone among the armed men, and they fought with one another for the stone till all lay dead upon the ground. Still King Æetes would not give to him the golden fleece; and the heart of Jason was cast down till Medeia came to him and bade him follow her. Then she led him to a hidden dell where the dragon guarded the fleece, and she laid her spells on the monster and brought a heavy sleep upon his eyes, while Jason took the fleece and hastened to carry it on board the ship Argo.

So Medeia left her father's house, and wandered with Jason into many lands — to Iolcos, to Athens, and to Argos. And wherever she went, men marvelled at her for her wisdom and her beauty; but as they looked on her fair face and listened to her gentle voice, they knew not the power of the maiden's wrath if any one should do her wrong. So she dwelt at Iolcos in the house of Pelias, who had sent forth Jason to look for the golden fleece, that he might not be king in his stead; and the daughters of Pelias loved the beautiful Medeia, for they dreamed not that she had sworn to avenge on Pelias the wrong which he had done to Jason. Craftily she told the daughters of Pelias of the power of her wondrous spells, which could tame the fire-breathing bulls, and lull the dragon to sleep, and bring back the brightness of youth to the withered cheeks of the old. And the daughters of Pelias said to her, 'Our father is old, and his limbs are weak and tottering; show us how once more he can be made young.' Then Medeia took a ram and cut it up, and put its limbs into a cauldron, and when she had boiled them on the hearth there came forth a lamb; and she said, 'So shall your father be brought back again to youth and strength, if ye will do to him as I have done to the ram; and when the time is come, I will speak the words of my spell, and the change shall be accomplished.' So the daughters of Pelias followed her counsel, and put the body of their father into the cauldron; and, as it boiled on the hearth, Medeia said, 'I must go up to the house-top and look forth on the broad heaven, that I may know the time to speak the words of my charm.' And the fire waxed fiercer and fiercer, and Medeia gazed on at the bright stars, and came not down from the house-top till the limbs of Pelias were consumed away.

Then a look of fierce hatred passed over her

face, and she said, 'O daughters of Pelias, ye have slain your father, and I go with Jason to the land of Argos.' So thither she sped with him in her dragon chariot which bore them to the house of King Creon.

Long time she abode in Argos, rejoicing in the love of Jason and at the sight of her children who were growing up in strength and beauty. But Jason cared less and less for the wise and cunning Medeia, for she seemed not to him as one of the daughters of men; and he loved more to look on Glauké the daughter of the king, till at last he longed to be free from the love and the power of Medeia.

Then men talked in Argos of the love of Jason for the beautiful Glauké; and Medeia heard how he was going to wed another wife. Once more her face grew dark with anger, as when she left the daughters of Pelias mourning for their father; and she vowed a vow that Jason should repent of his great treachery. But she hid her anger within her heart, and her eye was bright and her voice was soft and gentle as she spake to Jason and said, 'They tell me that thou art to wed the daughter of Creon; I had not thought thus to lose the love for which I left my father's house and came with thee to the land of strangers. Yet do

I chide thee not, for it may be thou canst not love the wise Colchian maiden like the soft daughters of the Argive land; and yet thou knowest not altogether how I have loved thee. Go then and dwell with Glaukê, and I will send her a bright gift, so that thou mayest not forget the days that are past.'

So Jason went away, well pleased that Medeia had spoken to him so gently and upbraided him not; and presently his children came after him to the house of Creon, and said, 'O father, we have brought a wreath for Glaukê, and a robe which Hêlios gave to our mother Medeia before she came away with thee from the house of her father.' Then Glaukê came forth eagerly to take the gifts; and she placed the glittering wreath on her head and wrapped the robe round her slender form. Like a happy child, she looked into a mirror [38] to watch the sparkling of the jewels on her fair forehead, and sat down on the couch playing with the folds of the robe of Hêlios. But soon a look of pain passed over her face, and her eyes shone with a fiery light as she lifted her hand to take the wreath away [39]; but the will of Medeia was accomplished, for the poison had eaten into her veins, and the robe clung with a deadly grasp to her scorched and wasted limbs.

Through the wide halls ran the scream of her agony, as Creon clasped his child in his arms. Then sped the poison through his veins also, and Creon died with Glauké.

Then Medeia went with her children to the house-top, and looked up to the blue heaven; and stretching forth her arms she said, 'O Hêlios who didst give to me the wise and cunning heart, I have avenged me on Jason, even as once I avenged him on Pelias. Thou hast given me thy power; yet, it may be, I would rather have the lifelong love of the helpless daughters of men.'

Presently her dragon chariot rose into the sky, and the people of Argos saw the mighty Medeia no more.[40]

KYRÊNÊ.

AMONG the valleys and hills of Thessaly
Kyrênê, the fair-armed daughter of Hypseus,
wandered free as the deer upon the mountain
side. Of all the maidens of the land there was
none to vie with her in beauty; neither was there
any that could be matched with her for strength
of arm and speed of foot. She touched not the
loom or spindle; she cared not for banquets with
those who revel under houses. Her feasts were
spread on the green grass, beneath the branching
tree; and with her spear and dagger she went
fearless among the beasts of the field, or sought
them out in their dens.

One day she was roaming along the winding
banks of Peneios, when a lion sprang from a
thicket across her path. Neither spear nor dagger
was in her hand; but the heart of Kyrênê knew
no fear, and she grappled with him until the
beast sank wearied at her feet. She had conquered, but not unseen, for Phœbus Apollo had
watched the fair maiden as she battled with the

angry lion; and straightway he called the wise centaur Cheiron, who had taught him in the days of his youth. 'Come forth,' he said, 'from thy dark cave, and teach me once again, for I have a question to ask thee. Look at yonder maiden, and the beast which lies beaten at her feet; and tell me (for thou art wise) whence she comes, and what name she bears? Who is she, that thus she wanders in these lonely valleys without fear and without hurt? Tell me if she may be wooed and won?' Then Cheiron looked steadfastly at the face of Phœbus, and a smile passed over his countenance as he answered, 'There are hidden keys to unlock the prison-house of love; but why askest thou me of the maiden's name and race,— thou who knowest the end of all things, and all the paths along which the sons of men are journeying? Thou hast counted the leaves which burst forth in the spring time, and the grains of sand which the winds toss on the river-bank or by the sea-shore. But if I must needs match thee in subtle wisdom, then listen to my words. The maiden is wooed and won already; and thou art going to bear her as thy bride over the dark sea, and place her in golden halls on the far-off Libyan land. There she shall have a home rich in every fruit that may grow up from the earth; and there shall thy son Aristæus be born, on whose lips the bright Horæ shall shed nectar and ambrosia, so that he may not come under the doom of mortal men.'⁴¹

Then Phœbus Apollo smiled as he answered, 'Of a truth, O Cheiron, thou deservest thy fame, for there are none to match with thee in wisdom; and now I go to bear Kyrênê to the land which shall be called by her name, and where, in time to come, her children shall build great and mighty cities, and their name shall be spread abroad throughout all the earth for strength and wisdom.'

So the maiden Kyrênê came to the Libyan land, and there Aristæus her child was born. And Hermes carried the babe to the bright Horæ, who granted him an endless life; and he dwelt in the broad Libyan plains, tending his flocks, and bringing forth rich harvests from the earth. For him the bees wrought their sweetest honey; for him the sheep gave the softest wool; for him the corn-fields waved with the fullest grain. No blight touched the grapes which his hand had tended; no sickness vexed the herds which fed in his large pastures. And they who dwelt in the land said, 'Strife and war bring no such gifts as these to the sons of men; therefore let us live in peace.'⁴²

BELLEROPHÔN.

THE minstrels sang of the beauty and the great deeds of Bellerophôn through all the land of Argos. His arm was strong in the battle; his feet were swift in the chase; and his heart was pure as the pure heart of Artemis and Athênê. None that were poor and weak and wretched feared the might of Bellerophôn. To them the sight of his beautiful form brought only joy and gladness; but the proud and boastful, the slanderer and the robber, dreaded the glance of his keen eye. But the hand of Zeus lay heavy upon Bellerophôn. He dwelt in the halls of King Prœtus, and served him even as Heracles served the mean and crafty Eurystheus. For many long years Bellerophôn knew that he must obey the bidding of a weaker man than himself; but his soul failed him not, and he went forth to his long toil with a heart strong as the sun when he rises in his strength, and pure as the heart of a little child.

But Anteia, the wife of King Prœtus, saw day

by day the beauty of Bellerophôn, and she would not turn away her eye from his fair face. Every day he seemed to her to be more and more like to the bright heroes who feast with the undying gods in the halls of high Olympus; and her heart became filled with love, and she sought to beguile Bellerophôn by her enticing words. But he hearkened not to her evil prayer, and heeded not her tears and sighs; so her love was turned to wrath, and she vowed a vow, that Bellerophôn should suffer a sore vengeance, because he would not hear her prayer. Then in her rage she went to King Prœtus and said, 'Bellerophôn, thy slave, hath sought to do me wrong, and to lead me astray by his crafty words. Long time he strove with me to win my love; but I would not hearken to him. Therefore let thine hand lie more heavy upon him than in time past, for the evil that he hath done; and slay him before my face.' Then was Prœtus also full of anger; but he feared to slay Bellerophôn, lest he should bring on himself the wrath of Zeus his father. So he took a tablet of wood, and on it he drew grievous signs of toil and war, of battles and death, and gave it to Bellerophôn to carry to the far-off Lykian land, where the father of Anteia was king; and as he bade him farewell, he said, 'Show this tablet to the king of Lykia, and he will recompense thee for all thy good deeds which thou hast done for me and for the people of Argos.'

So Bellerophôn went forth on his long wandering, and dreamed not of the evil that was to befall him by the wicked craft of Anteia. On and on he journeyed towards the rising of the sun, till he came to the country of the Lykians. Then he went to the house of the king, who welcomed him with rich banquets and feasted him for nine days; and on the tenth day he sought to know wherefore Bellerophôn had come to the Lykian land. Then Bellerophôn took the tablet of Prœtus and gave it to the king, who saw on it grievous signs of toil and woe, of battles and death. Presently the king spake and said, 'There are great things which remain for thee to do, O Bellerophôn; but when thy toil is over, high honour awaits thee here and in the homes of the bright heroes.' So the king sent him forth to slay the terrible Chimæra, which had the face of a lion with a goat's body and a dragon's tail. Then Bellerophôn journeyed yet further towards the rising of the sun, till he came to the pastures where the winged horse Pegasos, the child of Gorgo with the snaky hair, was feeding; and he knew that if he could tame the steed he should then be able to conquer the fierce Chimæra. Long time he sought to seize on Pegasos; but the horse snorted wildly and tore up the ground in his fury, till Bellerophôn sank wearied on the earth and a deep sleep weighed down his eyelids. Then, as he slept, Pallas Athênê came and stood by his side, and cheered him with her brave words, and gave him a philtre which should tame the wild Pegasos. When Bellerophôn awoke, the philtre was in his hand, and he knew that he should accomplish the task which the Lykian king had given him to do. So, by the help of Athênê, he mounted the winged Pegasos and smote the Chimæra, and struck off its head; and with it he went back and told the king of all that had befallen him. But the king was filled with rage, for he thought not to see the face of Bellerophôn again; and he charged him to go forth and do battle with the mighty Solymi and the fair Amâzons. Then Bellerophôn went forth again, for he dreamed not of guile and falsehood, and he dreaded neither man nor beast which might meet him in open battle. Long time he fought with the Solymi and the Amâzons, until all his enemies dreaded the stroke of his mighty arm, and sought for mercy. Glad of heart, Bellerophôn departed to carry his spoils to the home of the Lykian king; but as he drew nigh to it and was passing through a narrow dell where the thick brushwood covered the ground, fifty of the mightiest of the Lykians rushed upon him with fierce shoutings, and sought to slay him. At the first, Bellerophôn withheld his hands, and said, 'O Lykian friends, I have feasted in the halls of your king, and eaten of his bread; surely ye are not come hither to slay me.' But they shouted the more fiercely, and hurled their spears at Bellerophôn; so he stretched forth his hand in the greatness of his strength, and did battle for his life until all the Lykians lay dead before him.

Weary in body and sad of heart, Bellerophôn entered the hall where the king was feasting with his chieftains. And the king knew that Bellerophôn could not have come thither unless he had first slain all the warriors whom he had sent forth to lie in wait for him. But he dissembled his wrath, and said, 'Welcome, O Bellerophôn, the bravest and mightiest of the sons of men. Thy toils are done, and the time of rest is come for thee. Thou shalt wed my daughter, and share with me my kingly power.'

Then the minstrels praised the deeds of Bellerophôn, and there was feasting for many days when he wedded the daughter of the king. But not yet was his doom accomplished ; and once again the dark cloud gathered round him, laden with woe and suffering. Far away from his Lykian home, the wrath of Zeus drove him to the western land where the sun goes down into the sea. His heart was brave and guileless still, as in the days of his early youth ; but the strength of his arm was weakened, and the light of his eye was now dim. Sometimes the might was given back to his limbs, and his face shone with its ancient beauty; and then, again, he wandered on in sadness and sorrow, as a man wanders in a strange path through the dark hours of night, when the moon is down. And so it was that when Bellerophôn reached the western sea, he fell asleep and died, and the last sight which he saw before his eyes were closed, was the red glare of the dying sun, as he broke through the barred clouds and plunged beneath the sea.[48]

IPHIGENEIA.

THE ships of Agamemnon and the Achæan chieftains lay idle in Aulis on the narrow waters of Euripos. In vain they longed to reach the shores of Ilion and take vengeance on the treacherous Paris who had stolen away Helen from the halls of Menelaos at Mykênæ. Not a breath of wind stirred the sails on the masts; not a ripple on the sea moved the dark hulls of the ships. Then in his great strait Agamemnon the king bade them bring before him the wise seer Calchas, and he asked him if he knew wherefore they were made to tarry thus for weeks and months in Aulis. Then Calchas opened his mouth and told them of the wrath of Artemis, how she bare hatred to Agamemnon because once he had slain a stag in her sacred grove, and how she withheld the winds in the prison-house of Æolus until they should appease her anger by a rich offering. But when the soothsayer told them what the offering must be, then the two sons of Atreus smote with their staves upon the ground and lifted up their voices and wept aloud ", for the remedy seemed more terrible than the evil from which they sought to escape. Long time Agamemnon stood with his eyes fixed upon the ground, and his chest heaved with the greatness of his agony; but at length he spake and said, 'A hard fate is on me, O ye chiefs of the Achæans, for it is a fearful thing to shed the blood of my child to appease the wrath of Artemis; and yet how can I betray the men whom I have brought hither, and leave the ships to rot and our warriors to die for weariness and hunger?' But the seer gave no hope that the mind of Artemis would be changed; and the word was given that Iphigeneia must die. Presently the rumour ran through the whole army that the virgin child of Leto could not be appeased save with the blood of one as pure as herself; and all were filled with pity for the maiden, yet they cared not to change the judgment, because they longed yet more to avenge the wrongs and woes of Helen.

From the tent of Agamemnon came forth Calchas the seer with his servants, leading the maiden to the altar where the great sacrifice was to be done to Artemis. Hard by it stood King Agamemnon and Menelaos his brother; and the maiden sought, as she passed by them, to meet once more her father's eye; but his face was turned away and buried in the folds of his robe. He saw not his child as she looked towards him with a beseeching glance; he knew not how she sought in vain to speak a word, for the men who led her had laid their hands upon her mouth, that the voice of Iphigeneia might never be heard again. But while the priests made the victim ready for the sacrifice, the thoughts of Agamemnon went back to his home at Sparta, and he saw again his child in the freshness of her beauty, as she moved through his halls, bringing joy and gladness to all who looked upon her.

The words of Calchas were fulfilled, and the wrath of Artemis passed away. The soft western breeze rippled the waters of Euripos, and in a long line the ships of the Achæans sailed away from the shore to go to the land of Ilion. But the terrible Erinnys, who hovers in the air to see all the evil deeds which men may do, had not forgotten the sacrifice of blood in Aulis. Nine years they fought at Troy, and in the tenth the city fell, and the kingdom of Priam was destroyed utterly, as the sign of the dragon had taught them long ago when they were in Aulis.[45]

Then from cliff to cliff, across sea and river, from city to city, sped the tidings that the vengeance was accomplished and Agamemnon the king was coming back in triumph and glory. From hill to hill, across plain and valley, flashed the beacon fires; and before the first grey streak of dawn broke upon the eastern sky, the old warder who kept the nightly watch in the house of Agamemnon, saw the sign of victory and hastened to bear the tidings to Clytæmnêstra the queen. Then she said, 'The gods have dealt kindly with the hosts of the Achæans; make ready to receive the king as a conqueror should be welcomed.' And when she knew that at length Agamemnon was near at hand, she made ready embroidered tapestries and spread them on the ground, that so he might not touch the earth with his foot when he lighted off his chariot. Then she stood with downcast eyes to wait the coming of the king; and when he came, she welcomed him to his home with kind and gentle words. But her look was changed when in the chariot she saw a maiden seated; and Agamemnon told her that it was Casandra the daughter of Priam. Very fair was the maiden to look upon, but her face was worn with care and sorrow. 'She too is welcome,' said Clytæmnêstra, 'to the home of King Agamemnon.'

Then, as he stepped down from his chariot, Agamemnon said to Clytæmnêstra, 'Thy love hath carried thee too far, for thou art receiving me with honours too great for mortal man; and pride goes before a fall.' So he went on heedless to his doom. But to Casandra the Trojan maiden Phœbus Apollo had granted the gift of prophecy; only, because she would not give him her love, he added the judgment that none should believe her words. Presently a dark shade came over her face, and she clasped her hands as though from a sudden pain; and she cried out, 'Oh, what a sight dost thou show me, O Phœbus! In the bloodstained bath Agamemnon lies slain, as a wild bull in a net; and the dagger which has smitten him shall smite me also this day before the sun goes down.' But none gave heed to her wild cries until presently from within the house came a shriek loud and piercing, and then all was still again.

So the Atê of Iphigeneia came upon Agamemnon and brooded on his house, adding sin to sin and woe to woe. For the love of a child for his mother was dried up in the heart of Orestes, while he abode far away in a strange land; and when he grew to manhood and came back to Sparta, he slew his mother Clytæmnêstra, because she had killed his father. Then the Erinnys of his mother fell upon him and drove him in raging madness from the land. By day and by night they gave him no rest. He felt their cold breath on his cheek as he lay down to sleep, and he heard the hiss of the deadly snakes which were coiled in their tangled hair. Over hill and dale, from city to city, from land to land, they drove him with their pitiless scourge, till, faint of heart and ready to die, he fled to the sacred hill of Athênê. There in the solemn council, when the judgment was divided whether Orestes should live or die, Athênê gave sentence that he should go free. So the Erinnys of Clytæmnêstra fled away in grief and rage, and the Atê of Iphigeneia rested no more on the house of Agamemnon.[46]

HECTOR AND ANDROMACHE.

FAR away from the strife of battle, brooding over the wrongs which he had suffered, lay Achilles the son of Peleus; for Agamemnon had taken away the prize which the Achæans had set apart for him from the spoils of war. No more was his war-cry heard in the battle-field; and his spear smote not down the warriors who came forth to fight for Ilion. Then the other chieftains of the Achæans put forth all their strength in the battle against the Trojans; but the strongest and the bravest of all was Diomedes, the son of Tydeus. Wherever he came, his enemies fell back before him, till all trembled at the sound of his voice and the sight of his glittering spear. One after another fell the bravest and best of the Trojan warriors, until at last Helenos spake to Hector and said, 'O brother, the Achæans are pressing us hard, and the gods favour not the Trojans; what then shall we do, if they come not to our aid in the hour of need? Hasten, then, into the city, and gather the women together, and bid them go to the temple of Athênê and there beseech her with gifts and prayers that she may help the Trojans against the fierce Diomedes and the other chieftains who fight in the hosts of Agamemnon.' Then Hector answered and said, 'I will do thy bidding, my brother; but, O ye men of Troy, let not your hearts be cast down while I go to the sacred Ilion, and bid our matrons pray to the virgin daughter of Zeus to aid us in our need. It may be that she will hear our prayer; but if she hearken not, be not dismayed, for one good omen not even the gods can take away from men, when they fight for their home and the land in which they were born.' [47]

So Hector hastened to the house of Priam. Very fair it was to look at in the bright sunshine which streamed into the golden chambers. Then forth from the rich hall, where the king held banquet with his chieftains, came forth the lady Hecabê, leading her child Laodike to meet her brother. And when Hector came near to her, she took him by the hand, and called him by his name and spake in a soft and loving voice, 'O my son, wherefore comest thou hither from the battle-field? Are the men of Ilion so sore pressed in the fight that thou seekest the aid of the bright gods? Tarry yet a little while, and

I will bring thee wine to gladden thy fainting heart.'

But Hector said, 'Stay me not, O mother, for I have a great work to do; and if I tarry now by thy side, my heart may lose its strength, and my arm may fail me in the strife. But gather together the matrons of Ilion and bid them hasten to the shrine of Athênê and seek her favour by gifts and prayers. I go to the house of Paris, if so be I may rouse him to go forth against the enemy. Weak of heart, and mean of soul, he lies on his golden couch, and heeds not the evils which for his sake we are suffering. Of a truth, less bitter would be our sorrow if he were gone from the land of living men to the dark kingdom of Hades.'

So Hecabê parted from her child; and with the Ilian matrons she hastened to the temple of Athênê. With rich gifts and prayers they besought her aid, and Theâno, the priestess, placed on her knees a beautiful robe [46] which Hecabê had brought; and the smoke of the sacrifice went up to the high heaven, but Athênê hearkened not to their prayer.

Then came Hector to the house of Paris, and found him in his golden chamber burnishing his weapons and his armour. Near to him sat the

Argive Helen, and her handmaidens plied their tasks around her. Then Hector spake in grief and anger, and said, 'O Paris, idle and heedless thou sittest here, while the Trojan warriors are smitten down in the strife. Wouldst thou deal lightly by others who brought upon their country the evils which we bear for the sake of thee? Rise up and go forth to the battle, that our ancient city be not burnt with fire.'

But Paris answered gently, 'O Hector, I chide thee not that thou hast rebuked me, for well have I deserved thy reproof. Yet not in anger or in wrath did I forsake the people of my land; but my grief lay heavy upon me, and I sought to give myself up to my tears. But Helen hath prayed me to go forth to the fight; wherefore wait till I have put on my armour, or go thou first, and I will follow thee to the battle.'

But Hector stood silent and spake no word, until Helen spake to him softly and tenderly, and said, 'O Hector, brave of heart and kind of soul, never hast thou spoken a hard word to me who deserved all thy wrath. Ah, would that the dark wave had swallowed me as I came to Ilion in the ship of Paris from the city of Menelaos! then had I been at rest, and thou hadst not suffered all the evils which have come for my sake upon

the men of Ilion. But tarry here a little while,
and rest by my side; for great and sore is the toil
which thou hast borne for me in the fight against
the hosts of Agamemnon.' But Hector answered
hastily, 'Ask me not, O Helen, to tarry with thee
now. Thy words are kind and loving, but I may
not heed them. My people yearn for my coming,
wherefore do thou urge on Paris that he hasten
to put on his armour and meet me before I leave
the city. And now I go to my own home, that
I may greet my wife and my child before I depart to the battle, for I know not if I shall return again in peace from the strife of arms.'

Quickly he sped to his house; but the bridal-
chamber was desolate, and he heard not the voice
of Andromache among the maidens, as they plied
their tasks in the great hall. Then he said, 'Tell
me, O maidens, is Andromache gone to the homes
of her kinsfolk or the shrine of the pure Athênê
where the Trojan matrons are seeking by gifts
and prayers to win her favour?' Then one of
them answered, 'O Hector, if indeed I must tell
thee the truth, she hath not gone to her kinsfolk
or to the temple of Athênê; but she bade the
nurse bring with her thy child, and she sped, like
one on whom the hand of the gods lies heavy, to
the high tower of Ilion, because she heard that

the Trojans were hard pressed by the fierce Diomedes and all the chieftains of the Achæans.'

Then Hector tarried not to listen to more words. By the way that he had come he hastened again to the Skæan gates; and there as she ran to meet him he saw his wife and the child whom Hector called Scamandrios but the men of Troia called Astyanax, because of the great deeds of his father. There he stood still and looked gently on his child, but he spake no word; and Andromache took him by the hand, and, looking gently and fondly into his face, she said, 'O Hector, wilt thou hearken to my words? Sure I am that thine own brave heart will bring thee to thy ruin; and well thou knowest that thy death brings shame and sorrow to me and to our child. Ah, would that with thee I could go down to the dark land of Hades! for what hope have I when thou art gone? The fierce Achilles in one day slew my father and my seven brethren, when he took the sacred city of the Kilikians. Yet did he no wrong to the body of Eetion; but he laid him gently in the earth and raised a great mound above his grave, and the nymphs who dwell upon the mountains planted round it the clustering elm-trees. There, too, was my mother slain by Artemis in the halls of her father. . All are gone;

but, O Hector, in thee I have father and mother, and husband and brethren. Hearken then to my words, and abide with me on the tower, and let thy hosts stand beside the ancient fig-tree, where they say that the wall is weakest. And partly do I believe it, for why should there the Achæans make their fiercest onsets, if some one of the undying gods had not shown them that there they may scale the wall, and that thou heedest not its weakness?'

Then Hector strove to soothe Andromache and said gently to her, 'I have cared for all these things already; but ask me not to tarry here upon the wall, for never must the people say that Hector shrank from the battle-field. I must go forth to the fight, not as in the heedless days of youth, when men seek to win praise and glory, for my name is great already, and they call me the first among the warriors of Ilion. But well I know that we fight in vain; for the doom is fixed that the sacred Ilion shall fall, and Priam and his people shall be slain. But more than all I grieve for thee, and for the sorrows that shall come upon thee when thou art carried away captive to some far-off land. There, at the bidding of some Argive woman, thou shalt toil, and spin, and weave; and all who see thee weeping shall say,

"Look at the wife of Hector, who was the bravest of all the warriors of Ilion," and thy tears will be more bitter when thou hearest them speak my name, for the dark earth will lie heavy above me in the land of Troia, and I shall be far away from thee in the dark kingdom of Hades.'

So he turned to the babe who lay like a fair star in the arms of the nurse, and he stretched forth his arms to take him; but the child gazed fearfully at the long spear and the brazen helmet and the horsehair plume which waved proudly above it, and he shrank back with a cry, and nestled in the folds of his nurse's robe. Then Hector laughed, and took the helmet from his head and placed it on the ground, and the child feared no more to go to his father. Gently he took him in his arms, and he prayed aloud to Zeus and the undying gods that they would bless his child and make him glorious among his people, that so, in time to come, men might say, 'This man is stronger and braver than Hector.'

So he gave the child to Andromache, who received him smiling through her tears. The brave heart of Hector was moved with the sorrow of his wife, and he laid his hand gently on her and called her by her name, and said, 'Grieve not overmuch, O my wife, for none shall lay Hector low before the day of his doom is come. That day no man can avoid, be he good or be he evil. So let me go forth to the battle, and I will take heed for the guarding of the city; and do thou hasten to thy home, and there ply thine own tasks with thy handmaidens around thee.'

Then from the ground he took up his burnished helmet; and in grief and sorrow Andromache tore herself from his arms, and went slowly towards her home. Many a time she turned back to look upon him; but scarcely could she see the flashing of his armour, for the tears ran too quickly down her cheeks. So in silence and sadness of heart she entered her bridal-chamber, where she thought not to hear the voice of Hector again; and her handmaidens wept when they knew that once more he was gone forth to the fight, for they feared the wrath of Athênê and the strength of the mighty Diomedes.[49]

SARPÊDON.

WHEN Bellerophôn departed for the land of the setting sun, he left in Lykia a beautiful child named Laodamia, who became the mother of Sarpêdon. And when the Achæans came against the city of Priam to avenge the wrongs and woes of Helen, Sarpêdon took down his spear and shield from the wall and girded his sword upon his thigh, and went forth to do battle for the brave Hector against the hosts of Agamemnôn. Sadly he left the home where he had lived joyously with his wife and children; and there was mourning and sorrow in the house of Sarpêdon, for they thought that they had looked on him for the last time.

Then among the Trojan warriors fought Sarpêdon; and of all none was braver or more stout of heart than he. When others were faint of spirit, his voice still cheered them on; and the bright smile on his face roused them to fight more boldly for their country. If the hosts of the Trojans fell back in the strife, then Sarpêdon rebuked Hector with friendly words, and told him how he had come from the far Lykian land to fight for Priam, and had left his children and his wife behind him. He told him of all his wealth, and how he had left rich banquets and soft couches to do battle with the mighty Achæan chieftains.

Many fell beneath his hand; and of these none was braver and fairer than Tlêpolemos, the son of Heracles who had toiled for the mean Eurystheus and now dwelt with Hêbê in the halls of Olympus. Boldly he came towards him, exulting in the strength of his youth, and he chid Sarpêdon, and taunted him with shrinking back from the battle.

'Do they call thee a child of Zeus?' he said. 'What knowest thou of war and battles? My father Heracles came hither with six ships only, and destroyed the city of Ilion when Laomedon was king; and dost thou think to escape my arm?' But Sarpêdon said only, 'Thy father Heracles destroyed Ilion because the heart of Laomedon was not pure and he dealt treacherously with him by keeping back the reward of his toil; but I have no need to fear thee, and the day of thy death is come.'

So Tlêpolemos fell, and long time the Achæans were sore pressed, for the Trojans strove mightily to seize their ships. High above the din of battle was heard the voice of Hector; and Sarpêdon cheered on his men to the fight. Then said he to his kinsman Glaucos, 'Let none be matched with us for brave deeds. Are we not honoured more than all other men in Lykia; and look they not on us as on the bright heroes? The lands which they have given to us are rich with trees and corn; therefore must we do battle the more valiantly, that in after time men may say, "Our chieftains are rich and wealthy, and their garners are full and plenteous; but they fight for their people, and their name is great throughout the wide earth."' [50]

Fierce and terrible was the fighting day by day; and at night the blaze of many fires reddened the sky. But Patroclos came forth from the tent of Achilles, and the face of the battle was changed. Smitten by his spear, many of the bravest among the Trojan warriors were slain, and all were filled with fear as Patroclos drew near them in the fight. Then Sarpêdon said once more, 'Why shrink ye thus, O men of Ilion? I will go forth against him.' And he shouted his war-cry, and ran to meet Patroclos.

Then from his throne in the dark cloud Zeus looked down on his child Sarpêdon, and he spake to Hêrê the queen and said, 'Ah me, must Sarpêdon die, who is the dearest to me of all the sons of men; or shall I rescue him from the fight and bear him to his Lykian home?' Then answered Hêrê, 'The doom of Sarpêdon must be accomplished; and if thou drawest him away from the strife, then remember that other gods also have children among the hosts who fight round Ilion, whom they will seek to save from death. But if thine heart is grieved for Sarpêdon, still let him die by the hands of Patroclos, and, when his body lies dead, send Hupnos and Thanatos to bear him away to his far-off Lykian land, where his people shall mourn for him many days and lay him in the earth and raise a tomb over his sepulchre.' So Zeus hearkened to the words of Hêrê; but the big drops fell from the sky, because he was grieved for his child Sarpêdon.

Then Patroclos fought with Sarpêdon on the Ilian plain, and thrust his spear into his side, so that the life-blood gushed out. The darkness of death fell on his eyes, but his heart failed not for fear, as he cried, 'O Glaucos, brave friend and warrior, take thou my place, and cheer on the Lykians to the battle; and let not the Achæans have my body, for that were a shame to thee and to my people.' So died Sarpêdon, the son of

Zeus; and Glaucos was grieved at the heart, for he could not go to his aid, because his arm was torn with a grievous wound. Then he prayed to Phœbus Apollo the Lykian-born [51], and Phœbus drew the black blood from the wound and cheered the soul of Glaucos.

Fierce was the strife over the body of the Lykian king, until at length even the brave Hector was driven back and the Achæans took the bright armour of Sarpêdon. Then from the dark cloud Zeus spake to Phœbus Apollo and said, 'Hasten now, O Phœbus, and bear the body of my child Sarpêdon to the stream of Simoeis. There bathe it in the pure waters and anoint it with ambrosia and wrap it in shining robes, and then bid Hupnos and Thanatos carry it to the land of his people.'

So Phœbus Apollo bathed the body of Sarpêdon in the stream; and the round moon rose up from behind the dark eastern hills. No breeze whispered in the heaven above, no sound was heard upon the earth beneath, as the powers of sleep and death drew near on their noiseless wings. Gently they looked on the face of Sarpêdon, still and cold, but fair beyond the beauty which is given to the sons of men, before the toil of life is ended. Then they raised him softly in their arms, and the still air sounded not with the waving of their wings as they bore him homewards through the silent hours of night.

The first rays of Eôs quivered in the pale sky, as they laid the body of Sarpêdon in his own hall. Then was there sorrow and mourning for the great chief of the Lykians; but their tears were stilled as they looked on his face, so passing fair in the happy sleep of death. So they laid him gently in the earth and raised a great heap of stones above his grave, that in time to come men might tell of the great deeds of the good and brave Sarpêdon.

MEMNÔN.

FROM the burning land of the Ethiopians came Memnôn the fair son of Eôs, to aid the men of Troy against the Achæan chieftains. Like the brave and beautiful Sarpêdon, he was foremost in the strife of battle, and few might withstand the strength of his arm. Smitten by his sword fell Antilochos, the son of the old chieftain of Pylos. Bitter and deep was the grief of Nestor, the sweet-voiced speaker of the Achæans; and deep was the vow by which Achilles sware that he would avenge the death of Antilochos on the bright son of the Morning.

Then in the thickest fight Achilles sought out Memnôn, and he knew him by the height of his glorious form, and his beauty which was beyond the beauty of the sons of men. Long time they strove, but nothing might stand against the might of Achilles; so the son of Eôs was smitten down, and the heavy sleep of death fell on his eyes.

But Eôs saw her child die, and she came down to the earth and took away his body from the battle-field. In the pure waters of a river she washed away the dark blood, and wrapped it in a glittering robe. Long time she mourned, and her tear-drops fell on the earth whenever the sun rose up in the sky or sank beneath the waters of the sea. Then at last in bitter sorrow she hastened to the home of the undying gods, and fell before the throne of Zeus and said, 'O Zeus, look upon my grief, and give me comfort in my misery, for Achilles has slain my child, and the bright Memnôn lies pale and cold in death. If ever it hath been a joy to thee to look upon my face, when the first light of morning quivers in the sky,—if ever thou hast loved to see my glory spread its soft and tender flush before the path of the bright sun,—then let not my child wander among the dark shades in the land of Hades and Persephonê. Speak thou the word, and he shall come up in his brightness to gladden the heart of the undying gods.' Then Zeus bowed his head and spake the word; and Eôs wept no more, but hastened down to the earth; and Memnôn rose with her to the high Olympus, to feast with the undying gods in the halls of Zeus.[32]

ŒNONÊ.

THERE was sorrow, instead of gladness, in the halls of Priam, because a son was born unto him, and the lady Hecabê had dreamed a dream, from which the seers knew that the child should bring ruin on the Ilian land. So his mother looked with cold unloving eyes on the babe as he lay weak and helpless in his cradle; and Priam bade them take the child and leave him on rugged Ida, for the fountain of his love was closed against him.

For five days the dew fell on the babe by night, and the sun shone fiercely on him by day, as he lay on the desolate hillside; and the shepherd who placed him there to sleep the sleep of death, looked upon the child and said, 'He sleeps as babes may slumber on silken couches; the gods will it not that he should die.' So he took him to his home, and the child grew up with ruddy cheek and nimble feet, brave and hardy, that none might be matched with him for strength and beauty. The fierce wolves came

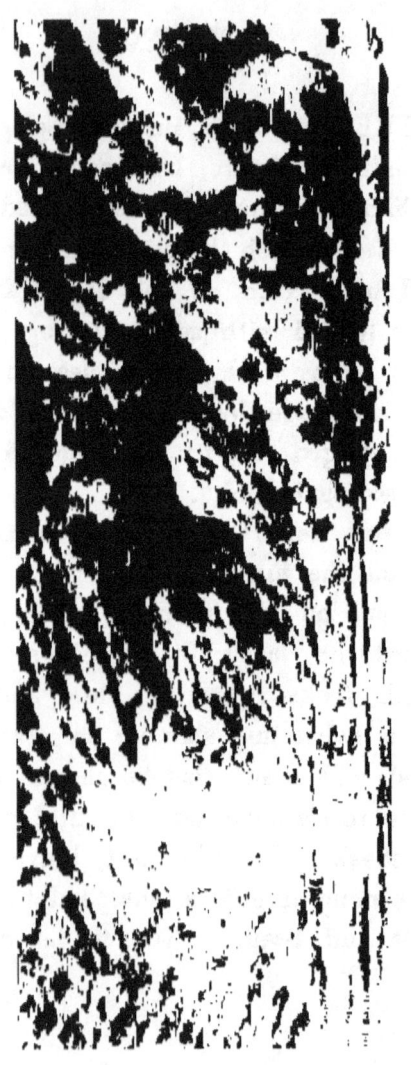

not near the flocks while Paris kept guard near
the fold; the robber lurked not near the homestead
when Paris sate by the hearth. So all sang of his
strength and his great deeds; and they called him
Alexandros, the helper of men.

Many years he tended the flocks on woody Ida,
but Priam his father dwelt in Ilion, and thought
not to see his face again; and he said within
himself, 'Surely my child is long since dead, and
no feast has been given to the gods that Paris
may dwell in peace in the dark kingdom of
Hades.' Then he charged his servants to fetch
him a bull from the herd, which might be given
to the man who should conquer in the games;
and they chose out one which Paris loved above
all others that he drove out to pasture. So
he followed the servants of Priam in grief and
anger, and he stood forth and strove with his
brethren in the games; and in all of them Paris
was the conqueror. Then one of his brothers was
moved with wrath and lifted up his sword against
him; but Paris fled to the altar of Zeus, and the
voice of Casandra his sister was heard saying, 'O
blind of eye and heart, see ye not that this is
Paris, whom ye sent to sleep the sleep of death on
woody Ida?'

But Paris would not dwell in the sacred Ilion,

for he loved not those who sought to slay him while yet he was a helpless child; and again he tended the flocks on the wide plains and up the rough hillsides. Strong he was of limb and stout of heart, and his face shone with a marvellous beauty, so that they who saw it thought him fair as the bright heroes. There, as he wandered in the woody dells of Ida, he saw and wooed the beautiful Œnonê, the child of the river-god Kebrên. Many a time he sat with the maiden by the side of the stream, and the sound of their voices was mingled with the soft murmur of the waters. He talked to her of love, and Œnonê looked up with a wondrous joy into his beautiful face, when the morning dew glistened white upon the grass and when the evening star looked out upon the pale sky.

So was Paris wedded to Œnonê, and the heart of the maiden was full of happiness; for none was braver or more gentle,—none so stout of heart, so lithe of limb, so tender and loving, as Paris. Thus passed the days away in a swift dream of joy, for Œnonê thought not of the change that was coming.

There was feasting and mirth among gods and men, for the brave Peleus had won Thetis the maiden of the sea to be his bride; and she rose from the depths of her coral caves to go to his home in Phthia. The banquet was spread in his ancient hall, and the goblets sparkled with the dark wine, for all the gods had come down from Olympus to share the feast in the house of Peleus. Only Eris was not bidden, for she was the child of War and Hatred, and they feared to see her face in the hours of laughter and mirth; but her evil heart rested not till she found a way to avenge herself for the wrong which they had done to her.

The gods were listening to the song of Phœbus Apollo as he made sweet music on the strings of his harp, when a golden apple was cast upon the table before them. They knew not whence it came; only they saw that it was to be a gift for the fairest in that great throng, for so was it written on the apple. Then the joy of the feast was gone, and the music of the song ceased, for there was a strife which should have the golden prize; and Hêrê the queen said, 'The gods themselves do obeisance to me when I enter the halls of Olympus, and men sing of the glory of my majesty; therefore must the gift be mine.' But Athênê answered and said, 'Knowledge and goodness are better things than power: mine is the worthier title.' Then the fair Aphroditê lifted her white arm, and a smile of triumph passed over her face as she said, 'I am the child of love and beauty, and the stars danced in the heaven for joy as I sprang from the sea foam; I dread not the contest, for to me alone must the golden gift be given.'

So the strife waxed hot in the banquet-hall, till Zeus spake with a loud voice and said, 'It needs not to strive now. Amid the pine forests of Ida dwells Paris, the fairest of the sons of men; let him be judge, and the apple shall be hers to whom he shall give it.' Then Hermês rose and led them quickly over land and sea, to go to the rough hillside where Paris wooed and won Œnonê.

Presently the messenger of Zeus stood before Paris and said, 'O fairest of the sons of men, there is strife among the undying gods, for Hêrê and Aphroditê and Athênê seek each to have the golden apple which must be given to her who is most fair. Judge thou therefore between them when they come, and give peace again to the halls of Zeus.'

In a dream of joy and love Œnonê sate by the river-side, and she looked on her own fair face, which was shown to her in a still calm pool where the power of the stream came not; and she said to herself, 'The gods are kind; for they have given to me a better gift than that of beauty, for the love of Paris sheds for me a wondrous brightness over the heaven above and the broad earth beneath.' Then came Paris and said, 'See, Œnonê, dearest child of the bright waters,—Zeus hath called me to be judge in a weighty matter. Hither are coming Hêrê the queen and Aphroditê and Athênê, seeking each the golden apple which must be given to her alone who is the fairest. Yet go not away, Œnonê: the broad vine-leaves have covered our summer bower; there tarry and listen to the judgment, where none may see thee.'

So Paris sat in judgment, and Hêrê spake to him and said, 'I know that I am the fairest, for none other has beauty and majesty like mine. Hearken then to me, and I will give thee power to do great deeds among the sons of men, and a name which the minstrels shall sing of among those who shall be born in long time to come.' But Athênê answered [63], 'Heed not her words, O Paris. Thy hand is strong and thy heart is pure, and the men among whom thou dwellest honour thee even now because thou hast done them good. There are better things than power and high renown; and if thou wilt hearken to me,

I will give thee wisdom and strength; and pure love shall be thine, and the memory of happy days when thou drawest near to the dark land of Hades.'

Then Paris thought that he heard the voice of Œnonê, and it seemed to whisper to him, 'Wisdom and right are better than power: give it to Athênê.' But Aphroditê gazed upon him with laughing eyes, as she came up closer to his side. Her dark curls fell waving over his shoulder, and he felt the breath from her rosy lips, as she laid her hand on his arm and whispered softly in his ear, 'I talk not to thee of my beauty, for it may be thou seest that I am very fair; but hearken to me, and I will give thee for thy wife the fairest of all the daughters of men.' But Paris answered, 'I need not thy gift, O child of the bright sea foam, for fairer wife than Œnonê no mortal man may hope to have. Yet art thou the fairest of all the daughters of the undying gods; and the gift of the fairest is thine.'

So he placed the golden apple in the palm of her snow-white hand, and the touch of her slender fingers thrilled through the heart of Paris as she parted from him with smiling lip and laughing eye. But Hêrê the queen, and Athênê the virgin child of Zeus, went away heavy and displeased; and evermore their wrath lay heavy on the city and land of Ilion.

Then went Paris to Œnonê, and he twined his arms around her and said, 'Didst thou see the dark countenance of the lady Hêrê, when I gave to the fairest the gift which the fairest alone may have? Yet what care I for the wrath of Hêrê and Athênê? One smile from the lips of Aphroditê is better than their favour for a whole life long.' But Œnonê answered sadly, 'I would that thou mayest speak truly, O Paris; yet in my eyes the lady Athênê is fairer far, and Aphroditê is ever false as fair.' Then Paris clasped her closer in his arms and kissed her pale cheek, and said nothing.

But the fierce wrath of Eris was not ended yet. Far away in the western land, there was sore famine in the kingdom of the mighty Menelaos; the people died by the wayside, and the warriors had no strength to go forth to the battle or the huntsmen to the chase. Many times they sought to know the will of the gods; but they heard only dark words for answers, till Phœbus Apollo said that the famine should never cease from the land until they brought from Ilion the bones of the children of Prometheus whom Zeus bound on the desolate crags of

Caucasus. So Menelaos the king departed from his home and went to the city of Priam. There he saw the beautiful Paris, and took him to the Spartan land, for he said that he should return home rich and wealthy. So Paris believed his words, and sailed with him over the wide sea. Long time he abode in Sparta, and day by day he saw the lady Helen in the halls of Menelaos. At the first he thought within himself, 'I would that Œnonê were here to see the wife of Menelaos, for surely she is fairer than aught else on the earth.' But soon he thought less and less of Œnonê, who was sorrowing for his long sojourn in the strange land, as she wandered amid the pine forests of woody Ida.

Quickly sped the days for Paris, for his heart was filled with a strange love and the will of Eris was being accomplished within him. He thought not of Œnonê and her lonely wanderings on heathy Ida; he cared not for the kindly deeds of Menelaos; and so it came to pass that, when Menelaos was far away, Paris spoke words of evil love to Helen and beguiled her to leave her home. Stealthily they fled away, and sailed over the sea till they came to the Ilian land; and Helen dwelt with Paris in the house of his father Priam.

But Œnonê mourned for the love which she had lost, and her tears fell into the gentle stream of Kebrên as she sat on its grassy banks. 'Ah me,' she said, 'my love hath been stung by Aphroditê. O Paris, Paris, hast thou forgotten all thy words? Here thine arms were clasped around me, and here, as thy lips were pressed to mine, thou didst say that the wide earth had for thee no living thing so fair as Œnonê. Sure am I that Helen hath brought to thee only a false joy; for her heart is not thine as the heart of a maiden when it is given to her first love; and sure am I too that Helen is not a fairer wife than I, for my heart is all thine, and the beauty of woman is marred when she yields herself to a lawless love. But the cloud is gathering round thee; and I see the evil that thou hast brought upon the land, for I am sprung from the race of the gods, and mine eyes are opened to behold the things that willingly I would not see. I see the waters black with ships, and the hosts of the Achæans gathered round the walls of Ilion. I see the moons roll round, while thy people strive in vain against the wrath of Hêrê and the might of the son of Peleus; and far away I see the flames that shall burn the sacred Ilion. I see thy father smitten down in his own hall, and the spear that shall drink thy life-blood. Ah me! for the doom that is coming, and for the pleasant days when we loved and wandered among the dells of woody Ida.'

So Paris dwelt with Helen in the house of Priam; but men said, 'This is no more the brave Alexandros,' for he lay at ease on silken couches, and his spear and shield hung idle on the wall. For him the wine sparkled in the goblet while the sun rose high in the heavens, and he cared only to listen to the voice of Helen, or the minstrels who sang of the joys of love and the bowers of laughter-loving Aphroditê. And Helen sat by his side in sullen mood, for she thought of the former days and of the evil which she had done to the good king Menelaos. Then there came into her heart a deep hatred for Paris, and she loathed him for his false words and his fond looks, as he lay quaffing the wine and taking his rest by day and by night upon the silken couches.

But throughout the streets of Ilion there was hurrying and shouting of armed men, and terror and cries of women and children; for the hosts of the Achæans were come to take vengeance for the wrongs of Menelaos. Yet Paris heeded not the prayers of his brethren, that he should send back Helen [54]; so she tarried by his side in his gilded chambers, and he went not forth to the battle, till all men reviled him for his evil love, because he had forsaken the fair Œnonê.

So for Paris fell the mighty Hector; for him died the brave Sarpédon; and the women of Ilion mourned for their husbands who were smitten down by the Achæan warriors. Fiercer and fiercer grew the strife, for Hêrê and Athenê fought against the men of Troy, and no help came from the laughter-loving Aphroditê.

Many times the years went round, while yet the Achæans strove to take the city of Priam, till at last for very shame Paris took from the wall his spear and shield, and went forth to the battle; but the strength of his heart and of his arm was gone, and he trembled at the fierce war-cries, as a child trembles at the roaring of the storm. Then before the walls of Ilion there was fiercer strife, and the bodies of the slain lay in heaps upon the battle-plain. Faint and weary, the people of Priam were shut up within the walls, until the Achæans burst into the gates and gave the city to sword and flame. Then the cry of men and women went up to the high heaven, and the blood ran in streams upon the ground. With a mighty blaze rose up the flames of the burning city, and the dream of Paris was ended.

Fast he fled from the wrath of Menelaos, and cared not to look back on the Argive Helen or the slaughter of his kinsfolk and his people. But the arrow of Philoctetes came hissing through the air, and the barb was fixed in the side of Paris. Hastily he drew it from the wound; but the weapons of Heracles failed not to do their work, and the poison sped through his burning veins.[53] Onwards he hastened to the pine forests of Ida, but his limbs trembled beneath him, and he sank down as he drew nigh to the grassy bank where he had tended his flocks in the former days. 'Ah, Œnonê,' he said, 'the evil dream is over, and thy voice comes back to mine ear, soft and loving as when I wooed and won thee among the dells of Ida. Thou hearest me not, Œnonê, or else I know that, forgiving all the wrong, thou wouldst hasten to help me.'

And even as he spake, Œnonê stood before him, fair and beautiful as in the days that were past. The glory as of the pure evening time was shed upon her face, and her eye glistened with the light of an undying love. Then she laid her hand upon him, and said gently, 'Dost thou know me, O Paris? I am the same Œnonê whom thou didst woo in the dells of woody Ida. My grief hath not changed me: but thou art not the same, O Paris; for thy love hath wandered far away, and thou hast yielded thyself long to an evil dream.' But Paris said, 'I have wronged thee, O Œnonê, fairest and sweetest; and what may atone for the wrong? The fire burns in my veins, my head reels, and mine eye is dim; look but upon me once, that, thinking on our ancient love, I may fall asleep and die.'

Then Œnonê knelt by the side of Paris, and saw the wound which the arrow of Philoctetes had made; but soon she knew that neither gods nor men could stay the poison with which Heracles had steeped his mighty weapons. There she knelt, but Paris spake not more. The coldness of death passed over him, as Œnonê looked down upon his face and thought of the days when they lived and loved amid the dells of Ida.

Long time she knelt by his side, until the stars looked forth in the sky. Then Œnonê said, 'O Eris, well hast thou worked thy will, and well hath Aphrodité done thy bidding. O Paris, we have loved and suffered, but I never did thee wrong, and now I follow thee to the dark land of Hades.'

Presently the flame shot up to heaven from the funeral pile of Paris, and Œnonê lay down to rest on the fiery couch by his side."[46]

THE LOTOS-EATERS.

AMONG the chiefs of the Achæans who fought before the walls of Ilion, there was none who gained for himself a greater glory than Odysseus, the son of Laertes. Brave he was in battle, and steadfast in danger; but most of all did the Achæans seek his aid in counsel, when great things must be weighed and fixed. And so it was that, in every peril where there was need of the wise heart and the ready tongue, all hastened to Odysseus, and men felt that he did more to throw down the kingdom of Priam than the mightiest chieftains who fought only with sword and spear.[57]

Yet, in the midst of all his toil and all his great exploits in the land of Ilion, the heart of Odysseus was far away in rocky Ithaca, where his wife Penelope dwelt with his young son Telemachos. Many a time, as the weary years of the war rolled on, he said within himself, 'Ah, when will the strife be ended, and when shall we spread our sails to the breeze, and speed on our way

homewards over the wine-faced sea?' At last
the doom of Paris was accomplished, and the
hosts of Agamemnon gave the city of Ilion to fire
and sword. Then Odysseus hastened to gather
his men together, that they might go to their
home in Ithaca; and they dragged the ships
down to the sea from the trenches where they
had so long lain idle.[58] But before they sat down
to row the ship out to the deep water, Odysseus
spake to them and said, 'O friends, think now,
each one of you, of his home, of his wife, and
of his children. Ten times have summer and
winter passed over us since we left them with
cheerful hearts, thinking that in but a little time
we should come back to them laden with glory
and booty. Ten years have they mourned for
us at home; and we, who set out for Ilion in the
vigour of our manhood, go back now with grey
hairs, or bowed down with our weary labour.
Yet faint not, O friends, neither be dismayed.
Think how they wait and long for you still at
home, and as we go from land to land in our voyage
to rocky Ithaca, let not weariness weigh down
your hearts or things fair and beautiful lead you
to seek for rest, till our ships are moored in the
haven which we left ten years ago.'[59]

With shouts of joy they sat down to their long

oars; and when they had rowed the ships out into the open sea, they spread the white sails to the breeze, and watched the Ilian land as it faded away from their sight in the far distance. For many a day they went towards the land· of the setting sun, until a mighty wind from the north drove them to a strange country far out of their course to Ithaca. Fair it was and peaceful beyond all lands which they had seen. The sun looked down out of the cloudless heaven on fruits and flowers which covered the laughing earth. Far away beyond the lotos plains, the blue hills glimmered in a dreamy haze. The trees bowed their heads in a peaceful slumber; and the lagging waves sank lazily to sleep upon the seashore. The summer breeze breathed its gentle whisper through the air, and the birds sang listlessly of their loves from the waving groves. Then said the men of Odysseus to one another, 'Would that our wives and our children were here! Truly Ithaca is but a rough and barren land, and a sore grief it is to leave this happy shore to go home, and there find, it may be, that our children remember us no more.' And Odysseus said within himself, 'Surely some strange spell is on this fair land; almost might I long to sit down and sleep on the shore for ever, but

Penelope waits for me in my home, and I cannot rest till I see her face once more.' Then he bade three of his men go forth and ask the name of the land and of the men who lived in it. So they went slowly from the beach where the waves sang their lulling song to the sleepy flowers; and they wandered along the winding stream which came from the glimmering hills far away, till, deep down in a glen where the sun shed but half its light, they saw men with fair maidens lying on the soft grass under the shade of the pleasant palm trees. Before them was spread a banquet of rich and rosy fruit, and some were eating, and others lay asleep. Then the men of Odysseus went up to them, and sat down by their side, for they feared them not, as men are wont to fear the people of a strange land. They asked not their name, for they remembered not the bidding of Odysseus; but they drank the dark wine and ate of the rosy fruit which the fair maidens held out to them. 'Eat,' they said, 'O strangers, of the fruit which kills all pain: surely ye are weary and your hearts are faint with sorrow, and your eyes are dim as with many tears. Eat of our fruit, and forget your labours; for all who eat of it remember no more weary toil and strife and war.' So they ate of the fruit, and then over their senses stole softly a strange and wondrous sleep, so that they saw and heard and spake even while they slumbered. On their ears fell the echo of a dreamy music, and forms of maidens, fair as Aphroditê when she rose from the sea foam, passed before their eyes; and they said one to another, 'Here let us sit, and feast, and dream for ever.'

Long time Odysseus waited on the sea-shore, and less and less he marvelled that they came not back, for he felt that over his own heart the strange spell was falling: and he said, 'Ah, Penelope, dearer to me than aught else on the wide earth, the gods envy me thy love; else would they not seek to beguile me thus in this strange land of dreams and slumber.' So he rose up, as one rises to go forth to battle, and he went quickly on the path by which his men had gone before him. Presently he saw them in the deep dell, and the rich fruit of the lotos was in their hand. Then they called to Odysseus and said, 'We have come to the land of the Lotos-eaters; sit thou down with us and eat of their fruit, and forget all thy cares for ever.' But Odysseus answered not; and hastening back, he bade the others come with him and bind the three men, and carry them to the ship. 'Heed not the people of the land,' he said, 'nor touch their rosy fruit. It were a shame for men who have fought at Ilion to slumber here like swine fattening for the slaughter.'

So they hastened and bound the three men who sat at the banquet of the Lotos-eaters; and they heeded not their words as they besought them to taste of the fruit and forget all their misery and trouble. And Odysseus hurried them back to the shore, and made them drag down the ships into the sea and sit down to their long oars. 'Hasten, O friends, hasten,' he said, 'from this land of dreams. Hither come the Lotos-eaters, and their soft voices will beguile our hearts if we tarry longer, and they will tempt us to taste of their fruit; and then we shall seek no more to go back again to the land of toiling men.'

Then the dash of their oars broke the calm of the still air, and roused the waters from their gentle slumber, as they toiled on their weary way. Further and further they went; but still the echo as of faint and lulling music fell upon their ear, and they saw fair forms of maidens roaming listlessly on the shore. And when they had rowed the ship further out into the sea, still the drooping palm trees seemed to beckon them back to slumber, as they bowed their heads over the flowers which slept in the shade beneath them. And a deeper peace rested on the Lotos land, as the veil of evening fell gently on the plain, and the dying sun kissed the far-off hills.[50]

THE CATTLE OF HELIOS.

FAR away down the gentle stream of Ocean [61], Odysseus had been to the dark kingdom of Hades and Persephonê, where the ghosts of men wander after their days on earth are ended. There he talked with Agamemnon and the wise seer Teiresias, with Minos and with Heracles; and there he had listened to the words of Achilles in the meadows of asphodel, and told him of the brave deeds and the great name of his son Neoptolemos. There the shade of Heracles spake to him, but Heracles himself was in the home of Zeus and lay in the arms of Hêbê, quaffing the dark wine at the banquets of the gods. And the shade told him of the former days, how all his life long Heracles toiled for a hard master who was weaker than himself, but Zeus gave him the power. Then Odysseus tarried no more in the shadowy land, for he feared lest Persephonê the queen might place before him the Gorgon's head which no mortal man may see and live. So he went back to his ship, and his men took their oars and rowed it down the stream of Ocean till they came to the wide sea; and then they spread the white sails, and hastened to the island of Æaea, where Eôs dwells and where Helios rises to greet the early morning.

From her home which the wolves and the lions guarded, the lady Kirkê [62] saw the ship of Odysseus, as she sat on her golden throne, weaving the bright threads in her loom. And straightway she rose, and bade her handmaidens bring bread and wine to the sea-shore for Odysseus and his men. Long time they feasted on the smooth beach, until they fell asleep for very weariness; but Kirkê took Odysseus to her own home, and bade him sit down by her side while she told him of all the things which should befall him on his way to Ithaca. She told him of the Seirens fair and false, and of their sweet song by which they tempt the weary seamen as they sail on the white and burning sea. She told him of the wandering rocks, from which no ship ever escaped but the divine Argo, when Jason led the warriors to search for the golden fleece.[63] She told him of the monstrous Skylla with her twelve shapeless feet, and her six necks, long and lean, from which six dreadful heads peer out over the dark water, each with a triple row of spearlike teeth, as she seizes

on every living thing which the waves of the sea
cast within her reach. She told him of Charybdis,
the deathless monster, who thrice each day hurls
forth the water from her boiling pool, and thrice
each day sucks it back. She warned him of the
Thrinakian land where the cattle of Helios feed
in their sunny pastures. There each evening as
the sun goes down, and each morning as he rises
from the eastern sea, the two fair maidens, Phaethusa and Lampetiê, come forth to tend them.
These children of Helios their mother Neæra,
tender and loving as the light of early day,
placed far off in the Thrinakian land to tend their
father's herds. 'Wherefore go not near that
island,' said the lady Kirkê, 'for no mortal man
shall escape the wrath of Helios if any hurt befall his cattle. And if thy comrades stretch forth
a hand against them, thy ship shall be sunk in the
deep sea, and if ever thou mayest reach thy home,
thou shalt return to it a lonely man, mourning
for all the friends whom thou hast lost.'

Even as she spake, the light of Eôs tinged the
far-off sky; and Kirkê bade Odysseus farewell, as
he went back to the ship. So they sailed away
from the home of the wise goddess, and they
passed by the Seirens' land, where Odysseus alone
heard the sweet sound of their singing as it rose

clear and soft through the hot and breathless air. Thence they came to the secret caves of Skylla; and her six heads, stretched out above the boiling waters, seized, each, one of the men of Odysseus, and he heard their last shriek for help as they were sucked down her gaping jaws. But they went not near the whirlpool of Charybdis, for Odysseus feared the warning of Kirkê.

The sun was sinking down in the sky as the ship of Odysseus drew near towards the beautiful island of Helios. The long line of light danced merrily on the rippling sea, and the soft breeze fanned their cheeks with its gentle breathing. Then spake Odysseus and said, 'Listen, O friends, to my words. Last night the lady Kirkê talked with me, and told me of all the things that should come to pass as we journeyed home to Ithaca. She told me of the Seirens, of Skylla and Charybdis; and all things have come to pass as she said. But most of all she warned me not to set foot on the island of Helios, for there his cattle are tended by the bright maidens Phaethusa and Lampetiê. Each day Helios looks down upon them as he journeys through the high heaven; and no mortal man may lay his hand on them and live. Wherefore hearken to me, and turn the ship away so that we may not come to this land.

Well I know that ye are weary and sick with toil, but better is it to reach our home wearied and hungry than to perish in distant lands for evil deeds.' Then was Eurylochos filled with anger, for he had forgotten how he alone would not enter the halls of Kirkê when all his comrades were turned into swine, and how he had himself warned Odysseus against her wiles. So he spake out boldly and said, 'O Odysseus, hard of heart, and cruel in soul, thou faintest not in thy limbs, neither is thy body tired out with toil. Surely thou must be framed of hard iron, that thou seekest to turn us away from this fair and happy land. Our hearts are faint, our bodies tremble for very weariness, and sleep lies heavy on our eyelids. Here on the smooth beach we may rest in peace, and cheer our souls with food and wine; and when the sun is risen, we will go forth again on our long wanderings over the wide sea. But now will we not go, for who can sail safely while the night sits on her dark throne in the sky? for then dangers hang over mortal men, and the sudden whirlwind may come and sink us all beneath the tossing waters.'

So spake Eurylochos, and all the men shouted with loud voices to go to the Thrinakian land. But when Odysseus saw that it was vain to hinder

them, he said, 'Swear then to me, all of you,
a solemn oath that ye will touch not one of the
sacred herds who feed in the pastures of Helios,
but that ye will eat only of the bread and drink the
wine which the lady Kirkê gave to us.' Then
they sware, all of them; and the ship came to
land in a beautiful bay, where a soft stream of
pure water trickled down from a high rock and
deep caves gave shelter from the dew of night.
Then they made their meal on the beach, and
mourned [63] over their six comrades whom the
monstrous Skylla had swallowed with her greedy
jaws, until sleep came down upon their eyelids.
But when the stars were going down in the sky,
and before Eôs spread her soft light through
the heaven, Zeus sent forth a great wind to
scourge the waters of the sea, and a dark cloud
came down and hid all things from their sight.
So, when the sun was risen, they knew that they
could not leave the island of Helios; and they
dragged their ship up on the beach to a cave
where the nymphs dance and where their seats
are carved in the living rock. Then Odysseus
warned them once more: 'O friends, hurt not the
cattle in this land, for they are the flocks of the
great god Helios who sees and hears all things.'

All that day the storm raged on; and at night

it ceased not from its fury. Day by day they
looked in vain to see the waters go down, until
the moon had gone through all her changes.
Then the food and the wine which the lady
Kirkê gave to them was all spent, and they knew
not how they might now live. All this time
none had touched the sacred cattle; and even
now they sought to catch birds and fishes, so that
they might not hurt the herds of Helios. Wearied
in body, and faint of heart, Odysseus wandered
over the island, praying to the undying gods that
they would show him some way of escaping; and
when he had gone a long way from his comrades,
he bathed his hands in a clear stream and prayed
to all the gods, and they sent down a sweet sleep
on his eyelids; and he slept there on the soft
grass, forgetting his cares and sorrows.

But while Odysseus was far away, Eurylochos
gathered his comrades around him, and began to
tempt them with evil words. 'O friends,' he said,
'long have ye toiled and suffered: listen now to
my words. There is no kind of death which is
not dreadful to weak and mortal men; but of all
deaths there is none so horrible as to waste away
by slow gnawing hunger. Wherefore let us seize
the fairest of the cattle of Helios, and make a
great sacrifice to the undying gods who dwell in

the wide heaven; and when we reach our home in Ithaca, we will build a temple to Helios Hyperiôn, and we will place in it rich and costly offerings, and the fat of rams and goats shall go up day by day to heaven upon his altar. But if he will, in his anger, destroy a ship with all its men for the sake of horned cattle, then rather would I sink by one plunge in the sea than waste away here in pain and hunger.'

Then with loud voices all his comrades cried out that the words of Eurylochos were good, and they hastened to seize the fairest cattle of Helios. Soon they came back, for they fed near at hand, fearing no hurt and dreading not the approach of men. So they made ready the sacrifice, and sprinkled soft oak leaves over the victims, for they had no white barley in their ship. Then they prayed to the gods, and smote the cattle, and, flaying off the skin, placed the limbs in order, and poured the water over the entrails; for they had no wine to sprinkle over the sacrifice while it was being roasted by fire. So, when the sacrifice was done, they sat down and feasted richly.

But Odysseus had waked up from his sleep; and as he drew near to the bay where the ship was drawn up on the shore, the savour of the fat filled his nostrils. And he smote his hands upon his breast, and groaned aloud and said, 'O father Zeus, and ye happy gods who know not death, of a truth ye have weighed me down by a cruel sleep; and my comrades have plotted a woful deed while I was far away.'

Then swiftly the bright maiden Lampetiê sped away to her father Helios, and the folds of her glistening robe streamed behind her as she rose to the throne of Hyperiôn. Then she said, 'O father Helios, the men of Odysseus have laid hands on the fairest of thy cattle, and the savour of their fat has come up to the high heaven.' Then was Helios full of wrath, and he cried aloud and said, 'O Zeus and all ye the undying gods, avenge me of Odysseus and his comrades, for they have slain my cattle whom I exulted to see, as I rose up into the starry sky, and whensoever I came down again to the earth from the high heaven. Avenge me of Odysseus; for if ye will not hearken to my prayer, I will go down to the land of King Hades and shine only among the dead.'

Then spake Zeus out of the dark cloud and said, 'O Helios, take not away thy bright light from the heaven, and forsake not the children of men who till the earth beneath; and I will send forth my hot thunderbolts, and the ship of Odysseus shall be sunk in the deep sea.'

Woful was the sight, as Odysseus drew nigh to the ship, and to his comrades who stood round the burnt-offering. With fierce and angry words they reviled each other, and they looked with a terrible fear on the victims which they had slain; for the hides crept and quivered as though still the life were in them, and the flesh moaned as with the moan of cattle, while the red flame curled up round it. For six days they feasted on the shore, and on the seventh day the wind went down and the sea was still.

Then they dragged the ship down to the water, and sailed away from the Thrinakian land. But when they had gone far, so that they could see only the heaven above and the wide sea around them, then the dark cloud came down again, and Zeus bade the whirlwind smite the ship of Odysseus. High rose the angry waves, and the fierce lightnings flashed from the thick cloud. Louder and louder shrieked the storm, till the ropes of the mast and sail snapped like slender twigs, and the mast fell with a mighty crash and smote down the helmsman, so that he sank dead beneath the weight. Then the ship lay helpless on the waters, and the waves burst over her in their fury until all the men were swept off into the sea and Odysseus only was left. The west wind carried the battered wreck at random over the waters; and when its fury was stilled, the south wind came and drove Odysseus, as he clung to the mast, near to the whirlpool of Charybdis and the caves of the greedy Skylla. For nine days and nights he lay tossed on the stormy water, till his limbs were numbed with cold and he felt that he must die. But on the tenth day he was cast upon the shore, and so he reached the island where dwelt the lady Calypso.

ODYSSEUS AND CALYPSO.

THE lady Calypso sat in her cave weaving the bright threads with a golden shuttle, when she saw a man thrown up by the waves on the sea-shore. So she rose in haste, and when she came to the beach, Odysseus lay before her stunned on the rocks, with his limbs numbed and stiffened with the cold. Gently she raised him in her arms and carried him to her home; and there she tended him by night and by day, while Odysseus yet knew not that he had been saved from the stormy sea.

When he awoke from his long sleep, he saw before him a fair woman who looked on him with eyes full of tenderness and love; and Odysseus half thought at first that he was again with the wise and beautiful Kirkê; but soon he saw that the face of Calypso was fairer and the light of her eye more soft and tender. At last he spoke in a faint and low voice, 'Lady, I thank thee for all thy care and gentleness; and now tell me, I pray thee, thy name and the name of the land in which thou dost dwell.' Then Calypso answered (and her voice was sweet as the sweetest music), 'O stranger, the gods call me Calypso, and I dwell alone in this fair island which is called Ogygia. But thou art faint and weak; tell me not now of thy sorrows, but rest here in my cave till thy strength comes back to thee again, and then thou shalt tell me the tale of thy sufferings.' So she put before him bread to eat and a goblet of dark wine, and Odysseus feasted with Calypso in the cave. And as he looked around he saw that a great fire was burning upon the hearth, and the sweet scent of cedar-wood and incense rose up from it.

So day by day Calypso tended Odysseus in his weariness, and day by day she spoke to him more gently and lovingly. She asked him not again of his sufferings, or whence he came and whither he was going; she cared not for aught else, if only he might abide with her in her lonely home [66]: and she feared to ask him of his toil and woe, lest he should seek to go to some other land. But the heart of Odysseus was far away in his own country, and he yearned to depart to Ithaca and be with his wife Penelopê and see his son Telemachos once more. Long time he hid his sorrows in his breast, for Calypso spake only of her love, and how that he should remain with her always in her glittering cave. But at last Odysseus fell down at her knee and besought her with tears and said, 'O lady, I thank thee for thy love and care; and now, I pray thee, let me go away in peace to my own home. My name is Odysseus, and my father Laertes is chieftain in the land of Ithaca. Ten years we fought at Troy, and for many years since the city of Priam fell have I wandered over the dark sea, because the mighty Athênê was angry with me. At her bidding Poseidon, the lord of the waters, sent a great storm and scattered my ships, and we were carried to distant lands and to savage people, to the land of the Lotos-eaters, the Cyclopes, and the Læstrygonians, till at last all our ships were shattered save one only, in which I sailed with the men that remained to me. But when we came to the island of Thrinakia, my comrades slew the fairest of the cattle of Helios, and offered sacrifice with them to the gods and feasted for many days. Then Helios besought Zeus in his anger, and a great whirlwind seized my ship, and all my men were dashed into the sea, and I only remain alive of all the great host which I led to Troy from Ithaca. Pity me, lady, for my great sorrow, and send me to my home; for year by year my wife

Penelopê looks for my coming and wastes away
in a secret grief, and if I go not back soon she will
die.' But Calypso said, 'Ah, Odysseus, what dost
thou ask? I cannot send thee to Ithaca, for here
I dwell alone and have neither ships nor men.
Yet wherefore dost thou so yearn to go to barren
and rocky Ithaca? What dost thou lack here
of all that thy soul may lust after? Here thou
canst share my riches, and here thou hast my love.
Think not more of Penelopê: long since she has
forgotten thee, and it may be that now her love
is given to another.' But Odysseus spake quickly
and said, 'O lady, thou knowest not what thou
sayest; sure I am that Penelopê has not forgotten
me, and that she loves me still as in the ancient
days. Ah, lady, thou art of no mortal race, and
thou knowest not the love of men and women.'
Then a look of anger passed over the gentle face
of Calypso, as she answered, 'Dost thou chide me,
O stranger, and wilt thou not give me thy love?
Urge me not in thy folly, for the anger of the gods
is terrible. Yet think not of my wrath, O man of
many toils and sorrows; rest with me in my home,
where no grief may vex thee, and I will charm
thy cares away by the sound of my sweet singing.
I can tell thee of the feasts of the gods in high
Olympus, of Hebe and Harmonia and the

laughter-loving Aphroditê. Rest, rest, Odysseus. What is thy home to thee, when my arm is round thee and my voice falls gently on thine ear? Think not now of toil and labour: rest, rest.

Then she sang with a low sweet voice, and the touch of her hand as it rested on his head brought down a deep sleep on his eyelids. At her bidding the happy dreams came and stood beside his couch [67], and whispered to him of new joys and the delights of more than mortal love. So she laid her spell upon Odysseus, and he feared to speak more of his home in Ithaca. Twelve moons passed through their changes, and still he abode in the cave of Calypso, listening to her sweet songs and soothed by her gentle love; but often, when the thought of his home came back upon his mind, he hastened to the sea-shore, and wept with bitter tears for his great misery, and yearned for the day when he might go to rocky Ithaca.

But, for all her great anger, Athênê loved Odysseus still, and she went to Zeus and told him of his hard lot, — how Calypso kept him by her evil spells in the island of Ogygia. Then Zeus called Hermês the slayer of Argus with the hundred eyes, and bade him go to the lady Calypso and command her to send Odysseus to his home. So Hermês bound his golden sandals on his feet, and took in his hand the staff with which he brings sleep on the eyes of men or rouses them from their rest. Then from the high Olympus he flew down to the earth beneath, and skimmed the waves of the sea like a bird, until he came to the island of Calypso. Quickly from the shore he hastened to her cave. The sun shone brightly from the high heaven; the trees cast their cool shade on the rock. The sea-birds rested with folded wings on the branches. Round the stems of the pine and the cypress the vine clung lovingly, and its long clusters of rich grapes hung before the opening of the cave; while four fountains gave forth their pure streams to water the soft meadows where the violet and the rose looked up into the blue sky.

As Hermês stood before the cave, he heard the sweet singing of Calypso, while she plied her task with the golden shuttle. In the cave the fire was burning upon the hearth, and the sweet smell of cedar and incense filled the air. But Hermês saw not Odysseus as he entered in, for he was far away weeping on the sea-shore. Then Calypso rose in haste, for she knew his face, and said, ' Wherefore comest thou thus to me with thy golden wand? If thou bringest to me a charge

from Zeus, tell me his will, that I may do it.'
Then before him she placed the food of the gods
and poured out for him the nectar wine; and
when Hermês had feasted merrily, he spake and
said, 'I come from the great Zeus, who bids thee
to send away Odysseus that he may go to his
home in Ithaca. Long time has he fought at
Troy, and grievous sorrows have fallen upon him
since he left the land of Priam; and it is not
the will of Zeus that here he should die far away
from his own people.'

And Calypso trembled as she heard his words,
and she said, 'O Hermês, hard of heart are the
gods of Olympus who grudge to us the love of
mortal men. So, when the rosy-fingered Eôs [68]
loved Orion, then Artemis slew him with her
unerring darts in Ortygia; and when Iasion was be-
loved of Dêmêtêr, he was smitten by the thunderbolts of Zeus. And now ye grudge me the love of
Odysseus whom I saved from the stormy water, as
he lay stunned and bruised on the sea-shore. I have
cherished him in my home, and I thought to make
him immortal as myself and free from the doom
of the sons of men. But the will of Zeus must be
obeyed, and I will not withstand it. If Odysseus
seeks to go away from my land, let him go; but
I cannot give him help, for I have neither ships

nor men.' But Hermês only said, 'See thou despise not the bidding of Zeus, lest he be wroth with thee in time to come;' and then he flew on his golden wings to the halls of Olympus.

But Calypso hastened to the sea-shore, and there she saw Odysseus weeping for his grievous sorrow that he might not return to his home. Gently she went towards him, and she laid her hand on his arm and said, 'Weep not, Odysseus. I have given thee my love, and I have sought for thine; but if thou carest not to give it, I will aid thee to build a raft, and thou shalt go hence in peace, with plenty of food and wine; and I will send a soft and gentle breeze which shall take thee to thine own land, since so the gods will who are mightier than I.'

But Odysseus was full of fear when he heard these words, for he thought that Calypso was speaking craftily, and he said, 'O lady, dost thou seek to entrap me by guile, when thou biddest me cross the wide sea on a raft, where even the great ships may not pass? Even at thy bidding I may not go, unless thou wilt swear that no harm shall come to me for following thy counsel.' Then Calypso smiled, and laid her hand gently upon him and called him by his name; and she sware by the waters of the Styx, and the broad earth, and the high heaven above, that she sought not to hurt him by her words; and she led him back to her cave and spread a rich banquet before him. Then as they feasted together she said, 'Wilt thou go away, Odysseus? If thus thy heart is fixed, farewell now and in the time to come. But if thou couldst know the sorrows which await thee before thou mayest see thy home, sure I am that thou wouldst not forsake me. Ah, Odysseus, I can make thee undying as myself, and thy wife Penelopê is not fairer than I. The daughters of men cannot vie in strength and beauty with the deathless children of the gods.' But Odysseus said, 'Be not angry, lady. Well I know that my wife Penelopê cannot be matched with thee for thy glorious beauty, for she is but a mortal woman, and thou canst not die or grow old. But even thus would I return to her and to my home; for my heart is wasted away while I yearn to see Ithaca once more. And if sorrows and storms await me still, I am ready to bear them. Many woes have I suffered in the years that are past; let these be added to their number.'

So, when Eôs spread her rosy fingers in the sky, Calypso arose and put a bright robe on him, and a golden girdle round his waist; and she placed a sharp axe in his hand, wherewith he cut down the wood for the raft, and Calypso helped him to build it. When four days were past the raft was ready, and Calypso parted from Odysseus on the sea-shore; and as he went away from the land, she looked on him long with a tender and loving gaze, and sent a soft and gentle breeze to carry him on his way. Then she went back slowly to her lonely cave.

But Poseidon was filled with wrath as he saw the raft of Odysseus coming near to the Phæacian shore; and he stirred up a great storm, so that the heaven was black with clouds and rain. Sorely was Odysseus tossed on the heaving sea, until his raft was shattered, and once again he was plunged in the raging waters. But from her green cave beneath the sea Inô the daughter of Cadmus heard his cry for help, and she rose up to comfort him under the wrath of King Poseidon. So Odysseus was gladdened by her words, and knew that now he should one day come to Ithaca; and he battled more stoutly with the angry sea, until, weary with pain and cold and hunger, he lay numbed and stiff on the Phæacian shore. There, as he slept amidst the bushes that grew high up on the beach, Athênê went to the house of King Alkinoös, and spake to his child Nausicaä [69], the fairest and purest of all the daughters of men; and Athênê brought her down to the sea-shore, that so she might save Odysseus, who had known so great grief in his long wanderings after the fall of Troy.

ATYS AND ADRASTOS.

TEN years had Crœsus reigned in Sardes, and all things had prospered to his hand. His garners were laden with grain, his folds were full of sheep, his houses were stored with gold and silver and all precious things. Among all kings there was none richer than Crœsus, and none more mighty. No sound of war and strife was heard in all his land, for he ruled his people gently, so that even the men whom he had conquered hated him not [70]; and Crœsus thought, in the gladness of his heart, that of all men he was the happiest.

Now about this time Solon the Athenian came into the Lydian land, for he had left his own country, because he had given his people good laws and he willed not that they should be broken. So he made his countrymen swear an oath that they would use his laws for ten years, and then he went away that he might not be compelled to alter them himself. So he came to Sardes, and Crœsus welcomed him gladly, giving him rich banquets and gifts of all good things. When he had been there three days, Crœsus bade his servants lead Solon through all the houses where his treasures were stored up; and when he had seen them all, Crœsus spake to him and said, 'I have heard of thy wisdom, O Athenian stranger, and how thou hast given good laws to thy people, and that thou art going now through many lands, to see the cities and ponder on the ways and the life of men. Tell me then, hast thou ever known a man whom thou wouldst call happy in all things?' This question Crœsus asked, thinking surely that he would be named as the happiest of all men; but Solon flattered him not, and named Tellos the Athenian. Then Crœsus turned sharply on him, and asked him why he named Tellos; and Solon answered, 'Because Tellos lived when things went well with the city, and his own children were good and fair, and he saw their children springing up and prospering steadily; and also because after such a life he died very gloriously, for there was a battle between the men of Athens and Eleusis, and he came to the aid of the Athenians and having put the enemy to flight died nobly, and the people buried him on the ground where he fell [71], and honoured him greatly.'

Then Crœsus thought within himself, 'Surely after Tellos he must think me the happiest;' so he asked Solon. But Solon named Cleobis and Biton, and said, ' These men lived in Argos, rich in goods and strong in body; and it chanced that there was a feast held in honour of Hêrê, but the oxen were not at hand to take their mother to the temple. So they placed her in the chariot, and drew it thither over forty and five furlongs; and the people at the feast marvelled at their strength, and held their mother happy that she had such children. Then she stood up before the shrine of Hêrê, and prayed the goddess to give to her children the happiest thing which mortal man may have. So the young men lay down there in the temple, for they were weary, and fell asleep and died; and so Hêrê showed that death is better than life, and that there can be no better gift for man than to die happily.'

But Crœsus was angry and sore displeased, and said, 'So then, O Athenian, thou holdest my happiness in so little account that thou hast not even thought me equal to men of low estate.' Then Solon answered, ' O Crœsus, dost thou ask me, who know that the gods are full of jealousy, about the happiness of man? In a long life there is much to be seen and suffered from which man would willingly turn aside; and in his threescore years and ten, there is not one single day which brings not with it some change or turn of things, so that man in all his life on earth has no sure abiding. And now, O king, thou art rich and wealthy, and all things thus far have prospered to thy hand, but happy I may not call thee until I learn that thy life has been happily ended; for the rich man is not wealthier than he who has only whereby he may live, unless he keeps all his wealth until the hour of his death. Many a rich man is very wretched, and many in humble estate have good fortune. So, then, in the case of all we must wait till they die; for the sum of human happiness is when a man is fair in person and sound of mind and limb, when no sickness vexes him and no evil chance annoys him, and when his children grow up fair and strong; but all these things together never fell to the lot of any man, and he who has had most of them and goes down to the grave yet having them, best deserves the name of happy. But everywhere we must look to the end; for the stateliest tree is often torn up by the roots, while yet it stands forth in the fulness of its beauty.'

Thus spake Solon; but his words displeased the king, because he had thought little of his wealth and treasures, and bade him wait till the end should come.

So Solon departed; and after he was gone, when Crœsus lay asleep in the night, there came a dream which stood over him [72] and warned him that Atys his son should be smitten by a spear and die. Now Atys was the pride of his father's heart, and Crœsus rejoiced to see his child braver and stronger than all his fellows, and going forth boldly to the chase, and coming back laden with booty. Another son he had, but he spoke not, for he was dumb; and it was a grief of mind to Crœsus that the fate should be upon the bright and fair Atys. But when he arose in the morning, he said nothing of the dream; only he took all the swords and spears that hung in the men's chambers, and put them where none might fall down and hurt his son; and then he made for him a marriage-feast, and gave him a fair bride, that Atys might forget his sturdy pastimes in the joys of love.

But while the marriage-feast was not yet ended, there came a man in great sorrow, and besought Crœsus to cleanse him from guilt, for his hands were stained with murder.[73] So Crœsus cleansed the stranger, and then asked him whence he came and whom he had slain. And the man said, 'I am Adrastos the son of Midas, and I slew my brother unwittingly; so my father drove me forth, and I have neither home nor money.' Then Crœsus spake to him kindly and bade him be comforted, saying, 'Thou hast come to the house of a friend where thou shalt want for nothing; and the lighter that thou canst bear this mishap, by so much it will be to thee a gain.'

Not long after these things there came men of the Mysians to Crœsus, who said, 'O king, we are sore vexed by a mighty boar who lurks in the clefts and dells of Olympus, and destroys our harvests, and hurts and slays all those who go forth against him. Help us, then, and let thy son Atys and thy chosen youths go forth with us that we may smite this monster.' But Crœsus answered them hastily, 'Think not of my son, for I cannot send him with you; he has married a wife, and his heart is fixed on his love. But I will send chosen men of the Lydians with all my dogs, and I will charge them to put forth all their strength, that so ye may destroy this wild beast from the land.'

But Atys had heard why the Mysians had come; and even while his father was yet speaking, he came hastily into the room, and said, 'O father, in times past it was my pride to go forth to the

battle and the chase, and it was a delight to
thee, also, that I came back laden with riches
and glory; and now thou keepest me away from
both, but wherefore I know not. Hast thou
seen in me either cowardice or faintness of heart?
or dost thou think that I can show myself now to
my comrades who praised me once for my bravery
and my strength? Nay, with what eyes will my
bride look upon me, if I pass my life as a woman
and touch neither sword nor spear? Let me go
forth to the hunt, or show me in calm and plain
speech that it is better for me to stay at home.'

Then Crœsus looked sadly on the face of Atys,
as he stood in all his beauty before him, and he
said, 'My child, I charge thee not with faintness
of heart, and it may be that I see in thee no
fault at all; but there came one night a dream
which stood over me in my sleep, and said that
thou shouldst be smitten by a spear and die:
therefore have I brought thee a bride, and held
for thee the marriage-feast, if by any means I
may save thee from the doom which hangs over
thee; and, indeed, thou art my only child, for I
look not on thy brother as on a living son, for
the fountain of his speech is closed.'

But Atys said, 'O my father, none can blame
thee for thy care and forethought, when such a

dream hath visited thee; but thou hast not read
its meaning right, for a boar hath neither hands
nor spear, and it cannot smite in the way of
which the dream forewarned thee. If indeed the
dream had said that I was to die by a tooth, then
were there some reason in thy words; but it talked
only of a spear-point. Let me go, then, for we
have not now to fight with men.' Then Crœsus
said, 'I will not gainsay thy words, my son; only
I pray the gods may prove them true.' And so
saying, he sent for Adrastos the Phrygian, and
charged him to guard his son. And he said, 'O
Adrastos, I welcomed thee when thou wast griev-
ing for a mischance, for which I reproach thee not;
I cleansed thee from thy guilt, I have fed thee at
my table; and now I ask of thee a requital for
my kindness, and sure I am that thou wilt not
think it a hard one. Go forth with my son to
this chase; thieves may fall upon him by the way;
be then at hand to guard him, if such a mishap
overtake him. Go, then, and win honour for thyself also. Thou art young still, and thy limbs are
stout and strong. It is not meet that a son should
fall behind his father.'

Then said Adrastos, 'O king, I had not thought
to go forth to the chase again; for it is not seemly
that such a man as I should mingle with those

who are gay and happy, nor have I the will to do
so. But to thee I owe a great debt, and therefore
will I go forth and guard thy son with all care. So,
then, be not cast down; my own pledge I give
thee, that thy son shall come back to thee in
health and strength even as he leaves thee.'

From the gates of Sardes the huntsmen went
forth in gladness of heart; and the sound of
song and laughter rose into the still morning air.
At their head rode the brave and fair Atys, and
the Phrygian Adrastos was by his side. Merrily
in the sunshine glanced the spears of all the train,
as they rode gaily on towards the brushwood
thickets which clothe the sides of the Mysian
Olympus. Soon they tracked the boar in his
hiding-place, and chased him through thicket and
marsh and plain, until at last he turned round to
bay, and there was a fierce fight, while each man
pressed forward that he might slay the boar and
win the glory himself. There in the throng,
Adrastos launched his spear at the boar, and
smote Atys the brave and fair; and the vision of
the dream was accomplished.

In haste and grief the messenger sped back to
Sardes to tell the king how Adrastos had slain his
son. Then the mind of Crœsus was maddened
with rage and sorrow; and his grief was the more

bitter because his son had been slain by the man whom he had cleansed from the guilt of murder. Then in his agony he called on Zeus the purifier to witness all the evil which the stranger had done to him, and on Him who guards the hearth, because unwittingly he had welcomed to his board the murderer of his child, and on Him who hears the oath of friends [74], because the man who swore to guard his son had smitten him with his spear.

But even while he yet prayed, the Lydians came bearing the body of Atys, and laid it down at the feet of Crœsus. Then with outstretched arms Adrastos drew nigh, and, kneeling down before him, besought the king to smite him for his evil deed; and he wrung his hands in agony, and said, 'O Crœsus, I came to thee with the guilt of murder, and thou didst cleanse me; I went forth to guard thy son, and my spear hath slain him. Slay me now, for life is hateful to me for all this misery.' Then, even in the bitterness of his grief and agony, the heart of Crœsus was moved with pity for Adrastos, and he said, 'O friend, I seek not more atonement, now that thou hast judged thyself to be worthy of death: and I know now that thou art not the cause of this sorrow to me, saving only that thy hand hath done the deed against thy will; but it comes from that

God who forewarned me of the end that was coming.'

So Crœsus buried the brave and fair Atys; and Adrastos the Phrygian lingered weeping till all were gone, and then he slew himself upon the grave.

Then Crœsus called to mind the words of Solon, and he knew now that they were true.[75]

NOTES TO TALES.

Note 1. Page 91.

IN the ordinary versions of this legend, Procris is made to yield, as it would seem, almost immediately to the words of Kephalos, when he appears before her in disguise. The essential part of the tale is the identity of Kephalos under his several forms, while the time during which the change takes place is of little consequence. By lengthening the absence of Kephalos, a difficulty is avoided which seems to rob the story of all its interest. Procris may be inconstant, but the purity of the morning dew cannot be sullied; and the variation, introduced for this purpose, maintains, rather than departs from, the original idea embodied in the tale.

Note 2. Page 91.

The example of Nausicaä, the daughter of the Phæacian king Alkinoös, would of itself show that the washing of linen was no unworthy task for a princess of the house of Erectheus.

Note 3. Page 91.

In the hymn to Dêmêtêr, that goddess is first seen by the daughters of Keleos, king of Eleusis, when they come to draw water from the fountain. See Tales from Greek Mythology, p. 4.

Note 4. Page 92.

Procris and Hersê are in fact merely different forms of the same name. *Prush* and *prish* in Sanskrit means to sprinkle, chiefly with raindrops, and Bopp connects the word with the Latin *frigere*, and our *frost*; while Hersê comes from the Sanskrit *vrish*, to sprinkle, and is seen again in the Latin *ros*, and Greek δρόσος. See also Max Müller, Comparative Mythology, in Oxford Essays for 1856, p. 54.

Note 5. Page 94.

If Eôs, or the morning, is represented here as the rival of the dew, in other legends, as in Daphnê (II.), she appears as avoiding, rather than seeking, the love of the sun.

Note 6. Page 100.

In the versions given by the collectors of mythical tales, Procris appears before Kephalos disguised as a man, and under that form demands and receives his love. The legend is not found in Homer, or even in later poets; and it is obvious that this feature, which represents too truly the state of Greek society during the historical ages, must have been introduced into the tale at a very late date. The whole tone of feeling and expression throughout the Homeric poems is utterly alien to a sentiment which sprang up between the heroic age and the earliest period which may claim anything like an historical character.

Note 7. Page 104.

Professor Müller has remarked (Comparative Mythology, p. 55) that the Greek myth of Kephalos was localised in Attica. The first meeting with Procris takes place on the eastern promontory of Hymettos: a straight line drawn westwards from this point would touch the Leucadian cape whence Kephalos sinks to sleep in the sea.

Note 8. Page 104.

Such expressions may perhaps be regarded as bringing into too great prominence a sentiment preeminently Christian. Undoubtedly the introduction of modern sentiment, of whatever kind, in the interpretation of Greek poetry or philosophy, is a danger which has not been avoided as carefully as it ought to be. Mr. Ruskin yields to the temptation when he says that Homer, while telling of the death of Polydeukes, still speaks instinctively of the earth as the giver and sustainer of life; and Mr. M. Arnold, in the same spirit, sees in the most trivial details and repetitions of Homer a uniform 'grand style,' which is the modern requisite for an epic poem. It must be admitted also that in this instance our modern sentiment attaches too great a force to one or two expressions in Greek poets, and chiefly to the beautiful passage of Pindar, Olymp. ii. 100, &c. Yet in this exquisite ode the poet seems to rise above other poets and moralists, not so much in the clearness with which he speaks of immediate retribution after death both to the evil and the good, as in the vivid colouring which he throws over the future joyous life of the righteous. If others seldom get beyond the negative freedom from tears and labour, he adds the brightness of a sun which never sets, and golden flowers on land and water, fanned by the breeze which comes from the gentle ocean stream. Compared with this warm and glowing life, the shades of Heracles and Achilleus in the Odyssey dwell in a cold and cheerless paradise. But there can be little doubt that the feeling of Pindar is both older and more true. The conviction of immortality would, in the ages of strict mythical speech, be almost unconscious; and the assumption of a happy immortality would be forced upon them by the necessities of their ordinary language. It is precisely that conviction which would be weakened, and finally give way before the indifference and scepticism of later ages, and which perhaps we may be permitted to bring out more prominently in legends which clearly belong to the earliest mythological age. It can scarcely be brought out more forcibly than in the speech of an Indian chieftain to Columbus, if we may only credit its authenticity. See Washington Irving's Life of Columbus, book vii. ch. 5.

Note 9. Page 107.

In mythical speech Daphnê, Eôs, and Iolê expressed the same idea. All these were said to come back in the evening to greet the sun who had journeyed companionless through the hot hours of the day. In Homer (Odyss. v. 300, &c.), Eôs closes, as well as ushers in, the day.

Note 10. Page 109.

This and the following tale are combined in the Homeric hymn to Apollo. It is obvious that we have in this hymn two poems, not one; and, indeed, no attempt has been made to cement the two together. The second hymn, which narrates his wanderings, follows abruptly, at the 180th line, the close of the first, which guarantees his permanent abode in Delos. See Mure's Critical History of the Language and Literature of Ancient Greece, vol. ii. p. 327. It may be remarked that the way in which Lêto addresses the island of Delos is an instance of the degree in which things inanimate were invested with life, though not with human personality. So in the Hesiodic Theogony (129, &c.), the poet speaks of the 'long hills,' as springing from the union of Ouranos and Gaia, without losing the consciousness that he is speaking of hills, not of persons. The amount of direct personification in Greek mythology is by no means so extensive as has sometimes been supposed. Compare Grote, History of Greece, vol. i. p. 2, with Max Müller, Comparative Mythology, p. 41. Such conceptions as Nereus, Gaia, Ouranos, scarcely carry with them any idea of personal existence.

Note 11. Page 111.

Here, as with the island of Delos in the preceding tale, Telphûsa, although she can feel and express anger, is not the nymph of the fountain, but the fountain itself.

Note 12. Page 113.

As with the myth of Endymion, the cattle of the sun receive more than one local habitation. In the adventures of Odysseus they are localised in the island of Thrinakia. See Tale No. XXVII. of the present volume, and Tales from Greek Mythology, p. 107.

Note 13. Page 117.

It might perhaps be rash to infer the later date of this legend merely from the high moral tone with which it concludes. The greater antiquity of the preceding legend would be proved by the fact that it speaks of the earlier festival at Delos as still in its glory. But these words of exhortation to the Cretan priests show conclusively the object for which the oracles were set up; and the length of time during which they retained their influence is a sufficient guarantee that, on the whole, that purpose was faithfully kept in view. See also the Tale of the Great Persian War, p. 303, &c.

Note 14. Page 118.

This tale simply brings together some incidents which are necessarily separated in the history of Herodotus (v. 101—105, vi. 113—120, viii. 32—39). The expedition of the Persians to Delphi is involved in great obscurity (see Tale of the Great Persian War, p. 359, &c.); but the legend brings out in wonderful clearness the mingled action of gods, heroes, and men. It forms the subject of a very animated poem by Mr. Freeman, in 'Poems Legendary and Historical.'

Note 15. Page 128.

The punishment of Atê, like the strangling of the serpents by the infant Heracles, belongs to an earlier period than that in which the toils of Heracles were catalogued. As in the Iliad, Atê is here simply the spirit of mischief, whether foolish or obstinate (Homer, Il. i. 412, &c.): she assumes a very different form in the hands of Æschylus, as the avenging destiny which broods over a house until the expiation for blood is accomplished. In like manner the force of μοῖρα is intensified in later thought, until finally ἀνάγκη is exalted to absolute omnipotence. Eurip. Alcestis, 968, &c.

Note 16. Page 129.

I have not hesitated to introduce into the legend of Heracles the beautiful apologue of the sophist Prodicos, preserved by Xenophon in his Memorabilia of Socrates, ii. 1, 21, &c. It is conceived, as is shown elsewhere (Introduction, p. 53), in the very spirit of that mythical language which called the idea of Heracles into being, while it goes far towards refuting the groundless calumnies brought against the Athenian sophists. In his admirable defence of these public teachers, Mr. Grote (History of Greece, vol. viii. p. 516, &c.) has justly expressed his astonishment that any one can be found who discerns an equivocal meaning in a picture of such pure and unselfish virtue. If the apologue of Prodicos has any meaning, it is that the object of virtue is not reputation, but the benefit of others,— not power and influence, but the answer of a good conscience.

Note 17. Page 134.

The numbering of the labours of Heracles was the work of an age subsequent to that of the epic poets. Homer knows of no such catalogue; but from the idea of Heracles as toiling for others, and not for himself, such legends would be multiplied indefinitely; and the ingenuity of a later time would, as in the epic cycle, be exercised in weaving them into a connected history.

Note 18. Page 137.

The legend of Heracles, like every other legend of Greek mythology, exhibits the peculiar character of the Greek mind. His birth and death, together with the greater number of his labours, are localised in various parts of Greece; but in no other sense can it be asserted (as in Dr. Smith's Dictionary of Greek and Roman Biography and Mythology, art. 'Heracles,' vol. ii. p. 400b) that the myth was developed on Grecian soil. The opinion of Buttman, who looks on Heracles simply as a poetical creation of the Greek mind, fails altogether to account for the points of resemblance between the Greek myth and that of other Aryan nations; while that of K. O. Müller, who deduces it from the consciousness of power innate in every man, leaves out of sight the essence of the tale,—the involuntary toil of one who is compelled to labour for a master weaker than himself. With a truer insight into the nature of the legend, Dr. Thirlwall (History of Greece, vol. i. ch. v.) perceived the connection between the labours of Heracles and the course of the sun; but he considers that the chief features of his life were borrowed from the Phœnician mythology. More recent research has only extended the ground of Dr. Thirlwall's judgment. The affinity of Greek with Eastern mythology remains; but the idea of borrowed wealth has been displaced by that of a common inheritance.

Note 19. Page 138.

That Homer knew of the death of Meleagros is evident from the statement in the catalogue, Il. ii. 640. But our ignorance of the way in which he might have related his death does not justify us in regarding the versions given by the fabulists as post-Homeric. By the evidence of language, the incident of the burning brand must have been known long before the time of Homer, and is a relic of the genuine solar legend, handed down in the common speech of the people; yet, like so many other legends, neglected by the epic poet because it did not suit his purpose to narrate it. It is most unsafe to argue against the antiquity of a tale from the mere silence of Homer. A few casual expressions give us hints of factions amongst the gods,— of conflicts between them and the giant Titans; while an epithet is the chief evidence that even in the Homeric theology Zeus was not the oldest of the rulers of heaven. But these incidents involve the whole legend of Prometheus; yet of that legend Homer says nothing. The truth is that the epic poet, naturally enough, made use of those legends, or parts of legends, which he found convenient, and amongst their many versions adopted that which best fitted in with his design. Thus Tlepolemos (see Tale No. XXIV.) tells of the vengeance which Heracles took upon Laomedon, but he says little of his other exploits, and nothing of his loves or of his death.

In the present tale I have endeavoured to weave together the Homeric incidents, with what seems to be the older version, into one consistent whole.

Note 20. Page 139.

See Tales from Greek Mythology, p. 25, &c.

Note 21. Page 148.

See Tale No. xxviii. p. 254.

Note 22. Page 149.

Hic situs est Phaethon, currus auriga paterni,
Quem si non tenuit, magnis tamen excidit ausis.
                                        Ovid. Met. ii. 327.

Note 23. Page 151.

This incident (Hesiod, Theog. 502) does not harmonise well with the Promethean tale as told by Æschylus. Mr. Grote has analysed the whole myth of Prometheus with great care (History of Greece, part i. ch. iii). But the main question to be determined is how far the picture given by Æschylus is his own invention, and whether he has 'really relinquished the antique simplicity of the story,' or restored it to its earlier form. As it stands, there can be no doubt that the idea of Æschylus (Prom. V. 440—507) is fundamentally opposed to the conception of the Hesiodic ages.

Note 24. Page 152.

Hesiod, Theog. 590—616; Works and Days, 59—104. In the latter poem the office of Athéné is to teach Pandora how to weave, — a task more in accordance with her character than that of simply placing a veil upon her.

Note 25. Page 157.

This is the version of the legend given by Æschylus, who clearly implies (Prom. V. 110) that the knowledge of fire was imparted to men for the first time by Prometheus. Among the many variations of this myth, the only one calling for special attention is that which makes Athéné the accomplice of Prometheus in the theft of fire.

and represents his tortures on Mount Caucasus as a punishment for his unlawful love for the virgin child of Zeus. This version implies that the love was returned; and the union of Prometheus and Athênê in this attempt to benefit mankind, against the will of Zeus, may throw some light on the original idea of the goddess, while it places a difficulty in the way of some modern theories.

Note 26. Page 165.

The groundwork of this tale is given in Homer (Iliad, i. 397—400). But the poet mentions no reason for the conspiracy, nor does he speak of any change as resulting from it in the government of Zeus. These additions are perhaps more in accordance with the varying conceptions of Zeus in the tragedies of Æschylus. In the Prometheus he is the merciless taskmaster: elsewhere he is the just and equitable judge. If he spoke of the same being, some cause was necessary to produce the change; and this passing hint in Homer may supply it. The complicity of Athênê here again calls for notice, as bringing her into direct conflict with the will of Zeus.

Note 27. Page 108.

The translation of Semelê from Hades is mentioned by Pindar in the same beautiful ode which paints so forcibly the paradise of the good. Olymp. ii. 40.

Note 28. Page 171.

This legend represents Dionysos in a character which bears a striking contrast to the gravity and majesty attributed to him in the Homeric hymn. There the wine through which the vessel floats, and the vine which suddenly enwraps the sailyards, attest his divinity to those who have made him a prisoner. For a further examination of the subject, see Grote, History of Greece, vol. i. pp. 38—50, where the later and more corrupt forms of Hellenic belief and worship are traced to Egyptian, Asiatic, and Thracian influence. The legend of Pentheus is chiefly valuable as showing, along with that of the Thracian Lycurgus, possibly also with that of Orpheus (Virgil, Georg. iv. 522), that the change was not accomplished without a vehement opposition.

Note 29. Page 172.

It cannot be necessary to refer to one of the most exquisite lyrical poems in the English language, in which Shelley sings of the flight of Arethusa from the heights of Erymanthos to the Ortygian shore, where love wakens in her when life is ended. Only the constant reading of the poems in which he dwells on Greek myths will reveal the astonishing insight which Shelley, by the strength of his personal feeling, obtained into the true character of that mythology.

Note 30. Page 175.

Σαφῶς Σιδηρῶ καὶ φέρουσα τοὔνομα. Mr. Grote considers the pun unworthy of a dignified tragedy. In this instance, possibly, Sophocles may have interpreted the name rightly; it is otherwise with his pun on the name of Ajax (Aj. 425).

Note 31. Page 177.

In Homer Tyrô becomes the wife of Cretheus. Mr. Grote thinks that the present version originated with Sophocles (History of Greece, vol. i. p. 148). As with many other legends, it is possible that several versions may have existed together without any attempt to reconcile their inconsistency.

Note 32. Page 178.

In this legend, I must acknowledge my obligation to Mr. Freeman's poem of 'Poseidon and Athena.'

Note 33. Page 179.

'The sunbeams are my shafts with which I kill
Deceit, that loves the night and fears the day.
All men who do, or even imagine, ill
    Fly me.'   Shelley, Hymn of Apollo.

Note 34. Page 181.

Sophocles (Œd. Col. 696, 700) seems to assign an equal value to both the gifts.

Note 35. Page 181.

'Ἀμβρόσιαι δ' ἄρα χαῖται ἐπιρρώσαντο ἄνακτος
κρατὸς ἀπ' ἀθανάτοιο.   Homer, Il. i. 529.

Note 36. Page 187.

The wish to retain as much simplicity as possible for the character of Ariadnê, furnished the reason for not adopting that version which saves the consistency of Theseus by representing him as compelled by Dionysos to give up the daughter of Minos.

Note 37. Page 190.

This, as well as the more common version, is given by Pausanias (ix. 31, 6). However curious may be the reason which he gravely gives for thinking that the flower was known before the death of Narcissus, it is not surprising that his description of the love of Narcissus for his sister implies that modern Greek sentiment which mars the ordinary version of the tale of Kephalos and Procris. (See note 6.)

Note 38. Page 190.

A hand-glass of steel, or other polished metal, sufficed for the needs of Greek and Roman maidens. The Hindoo women carry such mirrors attached by rings to their fingers. They are now of glass; but the fashion probably comes down from an earlier day.

Note 39. Page 190.

Compare the beautiful description of the death of Alethe in Moore's Epicurean.

Note 40. Page 197.

This is the legend which, stripped of every marvellous feature, is gravely taken by Herodotus, along with two other legends treated in the same way, as supplying connected causes for the great struggle between the Greeks and Persians in the generation immediately preceding his own. Tale of the Great Persian War, pp. 3, 207.

Note 41. Page 200.

Virgil (Georgic iv. 323, &c.) seems to reject the idea of immortality here attributed to Aristæus by Pindar (Pyth. ix. 3).

Note 42. Page 200.

Professor Max Müller (Essay on Comparative Mythology, p. 42) regards this legend as a specimen of genuine mythological allegory which, expressed in modern language, would be equivalent to saying, 'The town of Kyrênê in Thessaly sent a colony to Libya, under the auspices of Apollo.' With this myth he mentions many more in which the mere substitution of a more matter-of-fact verb at once divests a tale of its miraculous appearance. If the present tale shows to how late a time such mythological expressions were prevalent, the whole class to which it belongs is valuable as proving the extent to which actual allegory entered into Greek mythology. Here, under strictly personal forms, an event is described which Mr. Grote (History of Greece, vol. iv. p. 30) attributes to the middle of the seventh century b.c., 'so far as can be made out under much contradiction of statement.' The complete human personality of Kyrênê may be contrasted with the opposite way in which Pindar (Olymp. vii. 100, &c.) treats the legend of Rhodes. But the difference may be accounted for by the weaker personality of Hêlios as compared with that of Phœbus Apollo. The mythical idea of Hêlios still survived so far as to confine him to the local habitation of the sun. Phœbus, though still the lord of light, becomes a separate being, who may roam at will through the world. Hence there was not the same necessity to allegorise Rhodos, who, as wedded to Hêlios, still remains nothing more than an island.

$$\text{Βλάστεν ἰξ ἁλὸς ὑγρᾶς}$$
$$\text{νᾶσος· ἔχει τέ μιν ὁ-}$$
$$\text{ξειᾶν ὁ γενέθλιος ἀκτίνων πατήρ.}$$

And, if the poet goes on to speak of her children, his expressions refer almost wholly to geographical divisions of the island. See note 10.

Note 43. Page 206.

The legend of Bellerophon exhibits points of resemblance to many others. (See Tale of the Great Persian War, p. 318, note 2.) It is plain, however, that in its origin it belongs to the solar myths of Heracles and Endymion and Meleagros. In its general character (like the legend of Perseus and Andromeda, with a few others), it approaches more to the spirit of Scandinavian and Teutonic mythology. Bellerophon must be numbered with the mythic heroes of the Volsung tale and the Nibelungen Lied, Sigmund, Sigurðr, Gunnar, and Baldr. In all, the original type, although still visible enough, is more or less overlaid by details and incidents grouped around it by the peculiar genius of the people amongst whom they have been handed down.

Note 44. Page 208.

χθόνα βάς-
τροις ἐπικρούσαντας Ἀτρείδας δάκρυ μὴ κατασχεῖν.
Æschylus, Agamemnon, 200.

Note 45. Page 209.

Homer, Iliad, ii. 308—320.

Note 46. Page 212.

In the great trilogy of Æschylus nothing perhaps is more remarkable than the wonderful power with which he has united legends, not originally connected, into one harmonious whole. In the present tale, I have endeavoured to give some idea of that unity, which is founded quite as much on a profound theological conviction as on his own poetical instincts. Atê with him has lost her ancient character of mischievous folly (note 15), and is now the principle of divine vengeance, which, though late, never fails to bring home the sin of the transgressor, and which can never be appeased without a judicial expiation. That this is the one pervading thought and belief in the whole trilogy is plain (if other proof were wanting), from the fact that the poet has rejected every version which, by representing the sacrifice of Iphigeneia as not really accomplished, would convert the calamities of the house of Agamemnon into mere accidents not referable to a universal moral law.

Note 47. Page 214.

See the sentiment of Hector (Iliad, xii. 243), adopted in no sceptical spirit by Epameinondas. It is curious to remark the totally different interpretations given by the same men of the same omens, if only their own circumstances are changed. A notable instance is furnished by Nikias and his soothsayers, in the case of the eclipse which sealed the death-warrant of the Athenian army before Syracuse. See Grote, History of Greece, vol. vii. p. 433.

Note 48. Page 215.

On the light which this statement has been supposed to throw on the art of sculpture in the Homeric ages, see Thirlwall, History of Greece, vol. i. ch. vi. p. 233, &c.

Note 49. Page 221.

This incident in the great epic of Homer brings out with special prominence the notions then held on the problem of man's free will, and the Divine foreknowledge or rather predestination. Hector anticipates the destruction of Priam and his people as an absolute certainty, yet that knowledge does not interfere with his active energy, or with prayers for the aid of Athênê. He knows that present effort is his duty; the issue he is content to leave with a power over which mortal man has no control. He can look forward to the time when his wife and child shall dwell as slaves in another land; but the foreboding does not prevent him from doing all he can to defend them now. He gives in immediate action the only solution of the mysterious problem; and this portion of the Iliad is therefore invested with a deeper pathos and a more genuine human feeling than any other.

Note 50. Page 224.

The motives are so given, Homer, Iliad, xii. 310—328. It may be remarked that they attribute the wealth and power of the kings or chiefs to the voluntary action of the people. The Lykia of Homer was not, however, the birthplace of the great Lykian confederacy of later times.

Note 51. Page 220.

The character of Apollo, as the lord of light, first won for him the names of Δήλιος and Λυκηγενής, and then localised him in Delos and Lykia. It is the same with Endymion and his Latmian cave, with Pyrrha the wife of Deucalion, and a host of others.

Note 52. Page 220.

The name of Tithonos, the father of Memnon, must have retained something of its mythical force for the Greek, when he spoke of Eós as leaving his couch in the morning to bring back daylight to men. If, even when they thus spoke, they had lost the consciousness that Tithonos and Titan were the same, and that both were names for the sun, yet it is absurd to suppose that they thought or spoke of Eós, the morning, as leaving the couch of a Trojan prince who was the son of Laomedon, and a brother of Priam. But, as Professor Max Müller has remarked (Comparative Mythology, p. 53), because 'Tithonos was a prince of Troy, his son, the Ethiopian Memnon, had to take part in the Trojan war.' His mythical character is again shown by the tears of 'morning dew' which his mother sheds on his death.

Note 53. Page 235.

It is perhaps to be regretted that, in his beautiful poem of Œnone, Mr. Tennyson has followed the example of Ovid, by making Athênê, as well as Hêrê and Aphroditê, appear naked before Paris. So great a violation of mythical characteristics is perhaps not surprising in a Latin poet of the Augustan age; to a Greek it must have appeared quite inadmissible. It is true that the legends of Briareos, Pandora, and Prometheus are opposed to some modern theories on her attributes; but (however unfitting it may be in the case of Hére) to deprive Athênê of her seemly robes and so place her by the side of the laughing Aphroditê is to go against the whole conception of her character.

Note 54. Page 241.

The growth of an historical sense is strikingly shown in the eagerness with which Herodotus adopts the impudent forgeries of the Egyptian priests as the solution of a difficulty in the tale of Troy which he evidently regarded as insuperable. All his love for Homer, all his deep faith in a supernatural order of causation, cannot bring him to think that for ten long years a whole people chose to suffer the miseries of war rather than give up a woman whom they regarded as the cause of all their sufferings. This incredible folly is to him a sufficient justification for accepting the statement that Helen was not at Troy at all, but that she was detained in Egypt by order of the king (Herodotus, ii. 120). It must be noticed that in this instance Herodotus does not refuse to believe on account of any supernatural marvels. Even with regard to these, his faith is not altogether uncriticising (see Tale of the Persian War, pp. 268, 270). His unbelief of Homer here rests on the analysis of human motives, and he is proof even against the statement that the Trojan senators wished to give her up, but that her great beauty made them abandon their purpose, as soon as she came among them (Iliad, iii. 154, &c.). There can be no doubt that so great a change of sentiment would have been fatal even to the preservation of the Trojan legend, if it had not been defended by the safeguard of metre until it was committed to writing. The bulk of Vedic prose tradition is indeed greater than that of the Homeric poems; but the former was preserved orally, not only because there has never been a change of feeling regarding its statements, but because it has been specially intrusted to the keeping of a priestly caste. The

Sagas of Northern Europe would be more a case in point;
but the prose Njala of Iceland would never have survived
for Mr. Dasent to edit, had it been handed down orally,
and if the sentiment of a later day had come to discern
any violent improbability or incongruity in the narrative.

Note 55. Page 242.

The arrows of Philoctetes and the robe by which Medeia
avenges herself on Jason, come from Herucles or Hélios,
and are relics of the mythical phrases which described the
fiery action of a vertical sun. The idea of the poisoned
robe which was fatal to Herucles himself, was suggested
by his death-struggle with the blood-stained clouds of
evening.

Note 56. Page 244.

The variations in the tale of Paris and Œnoné are many
in number. Those in which the present story departs from
the ordinary version are suggested by Apollodorus and
Lycophron; and perhaps it may be said that there is nothing
in Homer inconsistent with them. It is certainly not
asserted that Paris had always been so worthless as he
shows himself during the time of which the Iliad professes
to give the history.

The lament of Œnoné has been versified by Professor
Aytoun, in his volume of Lays of the Scottish Cavaliers:
but the poem of Mr. Tennyson had scarcely left room for
another; and the only justification of the present story is,
perhaps, that it gives the whole legend, whereas Mr. Tennyson
confines himself to the judgment of Paris and the
mourning of Œnoné for his desertion.

Note 57. Page 245.

This is the conception of Odysseus as given by Homer.
It cannot be denied that the proximity of wisdom to craft

is betrayed even in the Iliad, and that Odysseus can boast of having assassinated a man with the most mean and cowardly stealthiness, without, it would seem, the faintest idea of the greatness of his treachery. But, on the whole, he exercises that legitimate influence, gained by power of thought and readiness of words, which was the guarantee of future Hellenic development, as its absence amongst Eastern nations gave the assurance of their hopeless bondage. But the character of Odysseus suffered during each succeeding generation, and, along with that of most of the Homeric heroes, underwent a miserable degradation, even in the hands of the best tragedians of Greece. (See more particularly Gladstone's Homer and the Homeric Age, vol. iii. p. 500, &c.) It must, however, be admitted that in Mr. Gladstone's eyes the contrast is heightened by his exaggerated estimate of the Homeric Achilles and Helen, if not of Odysseus and others.

Note 58. Page 240.

Homer, Iliad, ii. 151—154. There is probably nothing in the mythology of Northern Europe which answers to the Nostoi or return of the heroes from Ilion. But the kinsfolk of Gunnar carry on the strife in their own land. As soon as Brenhyldr or Helen is placed in another country, a foreign expedition is the result; and the necessity of return would naturally furnish a subject of almost inexhaustible richness for an age in which all such tales were received as so much veritable history.

Note 59. Page 240.

. It would be absurd to depreciate the deep and honest love which during his whole absence Odysseus feels and expresses for his home, and which grows altogether more intense as that absence is prolonged. But a protest must be entered when it is asserted that by this deep human

love the poet intended to signify the yearning of the soul
for its home in heaven, and the course of the Christian
warrior battling with fleshly temptations in his heavenward
journey. The poet had no such didactic or theological
aim; and certainly Odysseus, although exhibiting a marvellous power of self-restraint at all times when such
restraint was necessary, is no pattern of strict asceti-
cism. (See Tales from Greek Mythology, Appendix,
notes 20, 21.) This is evident not only in his determination
to listen to the Seirens' song, while he takes measures to
counteract its dangers, and in his indulgence of his appetite
when Hermes has provided him with a safeguard against
all evil consequences, but still more in the conditions of his
sojourn with Kirkê and Calypso, even while he went forth
daily to weep on the sea-shore, overcome by his inexpres-
sible yearning for his home.

Note 00. Page 251.

The choric song in Mr. Tennyson's 'Lotos-eaters' gives a
vivid picture of the feelings of men who have shared in the
Lotos-eaters' feast. It is, however, a philosophical analysis;
and the single expression of Homer ($\beta o \acute{v} \lambda o \nu \tau o$ $\nu \acute{o} \sigma \tau o \nu$ $\lambda \acute{a}$-
$\theta \epsilon \sigma \theta a \iota$) does not immediately suggest speculations on the
end and purpose of human life, although it may leave room
for them. In this episode the self-restraint of Odysseus is
conspicuous; but he was conscious of a great and pressing
danger, and conscious also that he had no charm or anti-
dote against it; and at all such times his self-control and
determined energy never failed him. Had Hermes been
present now with some preservative, doubtless Odysseus
would have been as curious to taste the fruit of the lotos,
as he was ready to feast with Kirkê or listen to the
Seirens' song.

Note 61. Page 252.

The ocean of Homer is not a sea, but a river, to which the poet gives the epithets applied to inland streams. With its deep yet gentle current it surrounds the earth, while it feeds the great seas which communicate with its mouths in the far East. No storms trouble the smooth flow of its waters, no tide raises or depresses its level; and the names by which the poet expresses its unbroken calm stand out in marked contrast with the words of evil omen which speak of the dangers of the sea. (Thalassa). For the Homeric geography see Gladstone's Homer and the Homeric Age, vol. iii. section 3.

Note 62. Page 253.

The previous legend of Kirkê, with that of the Seirens, has been told in Tales from Greek Mythology, pp. 00, 00.

Note 63. Page 253.

The passage of the Argo broke the spell, and the Symplêgades thenceforth remained firmly fixed in the sea.

Note 64. Page 254.

In the legend of the Pythian Apollo, these cattle have their local habitation near the Laconian Helos (see p. 113). Their pastures had once been in the blue fields of heaven.

Note 65. Page 257.

Homer, Odyss. xii. 308. Here, as elsewhere, the appetite of hunger and thirst is satiated before, as it would seem, they call to mind the loss of their comrades. Modern sentiment might question the sincerity of a grief which seldom, perhaps never, diminished the natural desire for food and drink. It may, however, be compared with Odysseus' yearning for his home, while yet he at least endures the love of Kirkê and Calypso.

Note 66. Page 204.

Though attended by their handmaidens, Kirkê and Calypso have none whom they call husbands. This difference in their condition from that of most of the gods may depend on a further distinction in the mythical ideas respecting them. They live, it would seem, even without the society of their kindred gods, unless when some special cause brings a messenger from Zeus.

Note 67. Page 267.

In Homer, the dream has a real personality, with good and evil dispositions. The hurtful Dream is sent by Zeus to the tent of Agamemnon (Il. ii. 0, &c.); nor is the Dream apparently less personal, or less capable of discrimination, which visits the couch of Xerxes after he has dismissed the great council of the Persians (Herodotus, vii. 12). Mr. Grote (History of Greece, vol. v. p. 14) has remarked that in this instance Herodotus betrays the weakened conviction of a later age by using the neuter ὄνειρον in place of the masculine ὄνειρος; but the latter is certainly used in the tale of Atys and Adrastos (Herod. i. 34). See page 278.

Note 68. Page 260.

It is not easy to think with Professor Newman (Reply to Professor Arnold on Translating Homer), that this epithet has a reference to the Eastern custom of tinging the eyes and fingers with henna. The custom may be as old as Homer, and may not have been unknown to the poet; but the whole notion of Eôs is so inseparably connected with the idea of morning or evening light, that such an explanation of the epithet becomes, at the least, superfluous. On such a supposition it is very difficult to understand why the epithet should be limited to Eôs only.

Note 69. Page 272.

For the episode of Nausicaä, see Tales from Greek Mythology, p. 75.

Note 70. Page 274.

It would seem that the Asiatic Greeks scarcely regarded their subjection to Crœsus as a conquest. The real oppression which followed the victories of Cyrus called forth a vehement but unsuccessful resistance.

Note 71. Page 275.

Thucydides (ii. 34) mentions this as a rare honour granted for their unmatched valour to those who fell at Marathon.

Note 72. Page 278.

See note 67.

Note 73. Page 278.

In the Homeric age, murder or homicide, although furnishing a legitimate cause for revenge to the kinsfolk of the slain or murdered man, was in no other respect an offence against society, and involved no necessity for a religious expiation. At least nothing of the kind is mentioned in Homer; and Mr. Grote (History of Greece, vol. i. p. 34), from the statement of Herodotus that the ceremonial of expiation was the same among the Greeks and Lydians, infers that the former borrowed it from the latter. It seems as easy to account for the change by the gradual expansion of thought and feeling on the subject. As long as murder was a matter for pecuniary compensation, there was nothing like a public prosecution for the crime; but the institution of the latter would seem to involve a notion of religious impurity, as well as the idea of an offence against society.

Note 74. Page 283.

The many offices and attributes here assigned to Zeus seem all to unite in one person. It may be said that in the language of the mythical ages there was more than one Zeus. The Zeus who reckons up the number of his earthly loves is certainly not the Being of strict truth and justice to whom Achilles instinctively addresses his prayer. But this distinction scarcely applies to the time of Herodotus.

Note 75. Page 284.

As in the legend of the Vengeance of Apollo (p. 118), the actors in this tale are mortal men; but it illustrates, more forcibly perhaps than any other, the belief of the Greeks in the ordering of human affairs by the gods. In fact, their whole religious philosophy may be said to be embodied in the beautiful story of the life of Crœsus. It brings out prominently the change which has exalted the Mœrœ or Fates into powers which neither Zeus nor Apollo is able to withstand. It exhibits, not less vividly than the book of Job (ch. xiv. &c.), the changes and chances of all mortal life; the jealousy of the gods against all excessive riches and excessive happiness; the retribution which visits the sins of the fathers upon the children, and which may close in darkness and woe the most brilliant and prosperous career. It shows also the old belief of the conditions essential to happiness, the extent to which material good fortune and natural advantages were held requisite to constitute a happy life. The conviction must have been both wide and deep, as the philosophy even of a later day sufficiently attests; but the very completeness in which it exhibits this scheme of belief, removes the tale from the province of history to that of legend or fiction. 'The more valuable,' says Mr. Grote (History of Greece, vol. iii. p. 207), 'this narrative appears in its illustrative character, the less can we presume to treat it as a history.' Nay, even with regard to the whole life of Crœsus, Mr. Grote thinks that 'the religious element must be viewed as giving the form — the historical element as giving the matter only, and not the whole matter, of the story,' and that 'these two elements will be found conjoined, more or less, throughout most of the history of Herodotus' (vol. iv. p. 266). It is curious to remark how Aristotle attempts to meet the difficulties involved in the Herodotean belief, and how far he still remains under the influence of the old philosophy. The definition of happiness, which precedes his analysis of human virtue, will, and action, cannot dispense with a certain amount of material prosperity (ἱκανῶς κεχορηγημένον τοῖς ἐκτὸς ἀγαθοῖς), and that not for a part, but during the whole of life (οὐ τὸν τυχόντα χρόνον ἀλλὰ τέλειον βίον. — Eth. Nic. i. 10, 15). Thus the great ethical teacher, scarcely less than the historian and the poet (Sophocles, Œd. Tyr. 1528), has to reserve his judgment in the case of each man until his part has been played out on the stage of life.

THE END.

By the same Author.

TALES FROM GREEK MYTHOLOGY.

In square 16mo. price 3s. 6d. cloth, gilt edges.

THIS book is intended for very young children; and perhaps no apology is needed for setting before children who will have to go through a classical education, at an early age, subjects with which they must make acquaintance afterwards. It is important that the first impressions should be agreeable, as well as consistent with the conclusions of recent researches into the common Mythology of the Aryan race. The Greek legends in this volume are given simply as tales such as they were held to be in the ages which followed on the period during which these myths were the common speech of the people. They are so narrated that the steps may be unbroken which lead from the simple acquaintance with these stories to that minute analysis of their origin and growth which the science of Comparative Mythology has enabled us to accomplish. The notes are designed to make the book serviceable for purposes of instruction as well as of amusement.

Select Opinions of the Press.

"MR. COX writes for little children in a way which little children can and do understand. If some of his expressions now and then seem too childish, we can only say that they actually do serve their purpose. Young children delight in the stories—elder children and even grown people do not despise them ..... Mr. Cox keeps his sounder and deeper learning for a few notes at the end. The stories themselves he tells in such a way that Phryxus and Helle, Cadmus and Europa, are made as pleasant and intelligible to children as Jack and the Bean Stalk—more so, we fancy, than the Toms and Maries, Herberts and Ediths, of the modern storybook with a purpose."
SATURDAY REVIEW.

"THIS little volume appears to us to be extremely well done. There is in it an amount of genuine simplicity, good taste, and correct scholarship which prove that Mr. Cox has studied his Greek classics to good purpose. As the perusal of Robinson Crusoe's adventures can scarcely fail to generate a love of the sea in the breast of a young reader of the male sex, so we cannot imagine that a child could hear the story of Endymion's sleep, or of Demeter's sorrow, as narrated by Mr. Cox, without longing to drink from the fountain-head which supplies the material for such delightful tales. The volume is specially intended for the use of very young children; but its beauty of style will gain for it a welcome from the scholar."
CRITIC.

"This is an admirable little volume. Those who require a work on Mythology that they can place in the hands of their children, will find Mr. Cox's book of Tales in all respects worthy of their support. The language is simple and lucid; and the selection has been made with much skill and judgment."
JOURNAL of EDUCATION.

"These tales are summaries of Grecian fable for the use of very young readers, who are told, in simple and attractive language, the tale of Proserpine, of Endymion, of Orpheus and Eurydice, of Europa, of Ulysses and Arion. The story of the Treasures of Rhampsinitus is appended by way of variation. Mr. Cox has constructed a most pleasant little volume out of these ancient yet ever fresh and glittering materials."
ATHENÆUM.

"It is not given to many men to write for children in a style that shall be delightful to the most intelligent among them. Mr. Cox is, undoubtedly, one of the few who can do so. These tales from the Greek mythology are all that can be desired for young children. They are told with that graceful simplicity and refined dignity which are inherent in the best old classic legends. It may seem strange to grandpapas of our day to hear little girls and boys talking as familiarly of Pallas Athené as of Cinderella's godmother, and to see the little creatures dramatising the story of Odysseus and Polyphemus as diligently in the evening as they dramatised that of Jack the Giant Killer in the morning. The Greek legends find immediate favour with very young children when told as Mr. Cox tells them; and partly for the reason which we just now heard given by a little girl of six years old, one of Mr. Cox's admirers: 'Oh! I like these Greek tales, because the Greek people make all their gods and fairies beautiful!' Mr. Cox is, we believe, quite right in his opinion, that you cannot too early give a favourable impression of the classical subjects which educated boys will come in contact with in their lessons. A child is not made more precocious by learning and loving the stories of the Homeric poems, than by taking delight in the wanderings of Sindbad, or the adventures of Puss in Boots. Mr. Cox has written a little preface to this book which shows how well he apprehends and can minister to the wants of the youthful intellect, always supposing it not perverted by contact with low-minded adults—whether servants or relations."
SPECTATOR.

"We give Mr. Cox our heartiest thanks for this excellent volume, which we recommend all parents, guardians, and teachers to procure, and to read before passing it on to some young friend. It will make its youthful readers in love with the fine poets of ancient Greece; and for such reading they will be better and happier and wiser."
SCOTTISH PRESS.

"Classical mythology has ever had a charm for the youthful mind, which, throwing aside the explanations of material laws, instinctively grasps the beautiful stories abounding in Greek and Latin Poetry: a charm which can never die or lose its freshness. Mr. Cox remarks that as a classical education is general, no apology is needed for familiarising the minds of young children with subjects of future study; while it is of importance that first impressions should be agreeable, and at the same time not inconsistent with the conclusions which have been reached by the science of comparative mythology. The various legends here selected are clothed with a tenderness and simplicity of manner which forcibly reminds us of the spirit of the originals; and we cordially thank the author for the pains he has taken in producing a volume which must be cordially welcomed not only by the young, but by many a paterfamilias whose grammatical knowledge has passed away, but whose mind will cherish to life's close the memory of these immortal inventions of the ancient poets."
MIDLAND COUNTIES HERALD.

"Mr. Cox's little book is, as many of our readers may know, by no means the first attempt that has been made to adapt Greek mythological stories to the use of English children; but it differs in several important respects from any book of the kind which we have hitherto seen. On the one hand Mr. Cox has gone much deeper into the philosophy of his subject than his predecessors; on the other hand, the tales, as told by him, are much simpler in form, and are intended for much younger children than any for whom the experiment has yet been made. These two apparently opposite things are probably not without a connection. It probably requires that a man should have made mythology a matter of profound study before he could venture to throw the time-honoured myths of Greece into so very simple a form as Mr. Cox has done......That Mr. Cox has succeeded in his attempt we can venture to affirm experimentally. The tales are delighted in by quite young children, to whom they are simply like any other pretty stories, while they are not despised by elder ones who already know something of Greek mythology and literature from other sources."
GUARDIAN.

London: LONGMAN, GREEN, and CO. 14 Ludgate Hill.

By the same Author.

THE
TALE OF THE GREAT PERSIAN WAR,
FROM THE HISTORIES OF HERODOTUS.

In fcp. 8vo. with 12 Woodcuts, price 7s. 6d.

THE narrative of the Persian War can scarcely be divested of its original form without weakening or destroying its vigour and beauty; and if presented in any other shape, it may satisfy the requirements of modern criticism, but it will not be the same history which rose before the mind of Herodotus. There are many translations of Herodotus, but no translation can be free from some at least of the many defects which are incidental to the work of expressing literally in one language the thoughts and feelings of another. The narrative of Herodotus is also interrupted by long episodes and complicated digressions; and it has been thought that the omission of such portions, not belonging immediately to his main subject, will give a more faithful and vivid idea of the general manner of the historian. The present volume is an attempt to reproduce in an English dress for readers generally, and without the restraints imposed on a professed translation, a narrative rich with all the wealth of Homeric imagery, and never perhaps surpassed in the majesty of epical conception. The narrative has been critically examined in the chapters appended to the tale.

Select Critical Opinions.

"THE plan of this little work is so happy in itself, and so admirably carried out, that its pages are probably destined to become equal favourites with schoolboys and grave scholars.... The vindication of Themistocles is a masterly essay. The histories of all truly great men belong not only to their own country, but to mankind at large; and the writer who, by a careful examination of facts and a cogent disposition of arguments, wipes off some of the besmirching dross which has hidden the pure gold of a character in many respects heroic, has certainly achieved no light or despicable task."
EDUCATIONAL TIMES.

"FOR somewhat older children, and for men and women of all ages, the Rev. G. W. Cox, favourably known by his pleasant little volume of *Tales from Greek Mythology*, has written the Tale of the Great Persian War from the Histories of Herodotus. This is the ancient story itself as it was told by Herodotus, freely and freshly reported, without the stiffness of too literal translation, with omission of the episodes and digressions, but with a fine sense of its true charm. The same tale that delighted thousands of old at the Olympic games, comes now, fitly arrayed in pleasant English dress. The little volume is a book for all."
EXAMINER.

"Mr. Cox is eminently qualified for the task he has undertaken, and his success demands our approval. He has penetrated deeply into the religious element which is so prominent in Herodotus; he has thrown a charm into the narrative which is sure to attract the young; and the modern dress in which the tale appears seems to bring the event so much nearer to our own times, that we feel a stronger appreciation of the reality of the scenes described."
JOURNAL of EDUCATION.

"The author of this book is not only a scholar but a man of fresh and vigorous fancy. He has selected from the stories of Herodotus a continuous tale of that early Persian War which will live for ever in the minds of Western nations, whose noblest ideas of patriotism and liberty are derived from the record of its final battles, Thermopylæ, Marathon, and Salamis. Every person who has read Mr. Cox's *Tales from the Greek Mythology* will be glad to hear of his new work. The former was and is the delight of children of five or six years of age. The first part of the present will be the most entertaining book in the world, for the time being, to youngsters of double that age. But both books are as pleasant reading to intelligent cultivated grown people as they are to children. If it be a valuable power to talk to little ones so as to enlighten and to elevate while you amuse them, then must Mr. Cox be reckoned among our good writers, whose works will not be forgotten in the next generation." GLOBE.

"Mr. Cox, it must be remembered, does not at all profess to reproduce the whole narrative of Herodotus. His object is exactly the opposite: it is to give the Tale of the Great Persian War without the digressions ... That the digressions of Herodotus run far wider of the mark than the digressions of Polybius, is part of the character of the man. The result is, that it needs a rather attentive reader always to catch up the exact thread of his narrative. And injudicious commentators have sometimes made matters worse. In such a state of things, it is a welcome sight to see a finished Greek scholar like Mr. Cox come forward to deliver the father of Greek prose literature from the cruel bondage of a barbarian prison. He gives us the Tale of the Great Persian War: that is, he gives us the main thread of the history without the digressions. It is not too much to say that, to an English reader, these omissions amount to little short of a restoration of the true Herodotus. In short, Mr. Cox, we cannot help thinking, produces something like what Herodotus would have produced, if he had not been obliged either to "the knowledge to himself, or to put it the text of one work. In so doing it seems to us, done Greek literature a valuable and opportune GENTLEMAN'S MAGAZINE.

"Mr. Cox's *Tales from Greek Mythology* abundantly proved his power to translate Greek into such English narrative as children may usefully employ to gratify their taste for the marvellous. His *Tale of the Great Persian War* is a larger effort in the same line, and not less conscientiously performed. Entering thoroughly into the piety and simple honesty of Herodotus, Mr. Cox tells the tale as the great historian has told it, with all its marvels. He adds, however, an appendix of critical essays on some points of historical doubt, suited to more learned readers." GUARDIAN.

"Mr. Cox's book consists of two parts. In the first he tells, as a story, the narrative of the Persian War, as given by Herodotus—in other words, the history of Herodotus without the digressions. Here is a tale which may be read with interest simply as a tale, and which may also be useful to students of any sort as giving the essential and connected narrative without the constant divergences from the main story. The second part consists of a thorough critical examination of the credibility of the history of Herodotus, which, of course, addresses itself only to scholars, and which is well worthy of the attention of scholars. In his former part Mr. Cox simply narrates, after Herodotus, without criticising—he tells the immortal tale as it is told to him. In the second, he brings his sound scholarship and keen historical instinct to produce results which at first sight strike us as almost too sceptical. Mr. Cox unites several qualities which are in no way inconsistent, but which are not very often found together. He has a poetic sense which makes him thoroughly appreciate all the beauties of the story—a sort of dramatic power, which enables him thoroughly to enter into the position of the historian in telling his tale—and finally, an historic sense, which some may think is too unsparingly applied, as it leads him to reject as matter of fact much that he has just told with the keenest appreciation of its literary beauty. He thus stands distinguished alike from illogical admirers, who think it sacrilegious to doubt the literal truth of anything which pleases the imagination, and from mere dull critics, capable, it may be, of weighing evidence, but incapable of entering into poetical beauty. Mr. Cox holds that we may refuse a literal belief to large portions of the history of Herodotus without in any way diminishing our admiration for him as a narrator, or even our confidence in his thorough personal trustworthiness. And even if in some cases he seems to us, at first sight, to err on the side of unbelief, it may be simply because of the novelty of some of the questions which he starts, and we feel quite certain that he has hit upon what is essentially the right method of handling his subject."
SATURDAY REVIEW.

ndon: LONGMAN, GREEN, and CO. 14 Ludgate Hill.

www.ingramcontent.com/pod-product-compliance
Lightning Source LLC
Chambersburg PA
CBHW021153230426
43667CB00006B/380